Bastards

Management Advice You Should Have Been
Given Long Ago

KENNETH KOCH

iUniverse, Inc.
Bloomington

Bastards
Management Advice You Should Have Been Given Long Ago

iUniverse books may be ordered through booksellers or by contacting:

iUniverse
1663 Liberty Drive
Bloomington, IN 47403
www.iuniverse.com
1-800-Authors (1-800-288-4677)

Because of the dynamic nature of the Internet, any web addresses or links contained in this book may have changed since publication and may no longer be valid. The views expressed in this work are solely those of the author and do not necessarily reflect the views of the publisher, and the publisher hereby disclaims any responsibility for them.

Any people depicted in stock imagery provided by Thinkstock are models, and such images are being used for illustrative purposes only.

Certain stock imagery © Thinkstock.

ISBN: 978-1-4620-0597-0 (sc)
ISBN: 978-1-4620-0598-7 (ebook)

Printed in the United States of America

iUniverse rev. date: 3/22/2011

Contents

Acknowledgments

I'll begin by thanking each person who made this book possible, as they are the epitome of ghastly management. Without terrible managers like Gina, Lee Ann, Larry, and Jeff, this project may have never taken shape. Throughout our careers, we often wonder why we were placed in situations we had to put up with, but the culmination of this endeavor is proof that anyone can make lemonade out of the lemons they are given. It is because of you that I was able to realize this dream of offering something more to others, with the hope that I could possibly make a genuine difference in someone's career. By applying some of the ideas I have presented throughout this text, others may have an opportunity to realize career ambitions that I often visualize for myself.

I'd also like to thank Ashley Stinnett, whose personal writing pursuits served as a source of encouragement for me. As I watched you work to complete your projects, while encouraging me to remove the obstacles that prevented me from moving forward with my own, I developed a deeper appreciation of having people around that have the same "can do" attitude that I have. Although I sometimes lost that mind-set, your encouragement helped me find my way again.

And to Dianne and the boys, Mom and Jack, and my true friends who didn't laugh when I said I wanted to take on this type of assignment, thank you. This book is a credit and testimony to your belief in me. I hope I don't let you down.

Foreword

Most of the time, business books play nice. The authors of those books go out of their way to be diplomatic and politically correct so as to avoid all possibility of offending someone. After all, (as the apparent logic goes), if you offend the business world (your potential audience), then you risk having your books remain on the shelves at the bookstore. Obviously (as any good student of business knows), the objective is to sell books. Therefore, the order of the day is to offend no one. Unfortunately, the unintended result of this "kid glove" approach is that the message becomes so watered down that its significance and impact are obscured or lost completely. Readers who bought the book seeking guidance on how to improve their skills get a sterile reminder of the basics that they learned years before and a confusing description of management behavior that seems to affirm any and all management styles, techniques, and decisions. The corporate "bad guys" go away with a quasi "atta-boy," while conscientious managers, who were looking for solid principles upon which to build a career, go away more confused than ever. Or they put down the half-read book and feel frustrated and isolated.

Every once in a while, however, there is a clear voice that can be heard above the chaos. This voice delivers a message that is easily understandable and leaves no doubt about what is good and what is not. The owner of this voice is a leader. A leader is always confident, unyielding, and persistent, and (if necessary) is not afraid to offend. Kenny Koch is such a person, and he speaks with a strong voice. *Bastards* is a hard-hitting book that takes on several of the beliefs and behaviors displayed by today's managers. There is no candy-coating here, no hidden message. This book takes on some common workplace behaviors with uncommon clarity and frankness. Gone are the usual attempts to protect the feelings of the reader, and in its place are the words of someone who truly cares about your future. If your child ran into traffic, I doubt you would care much about political correctness. You would act quickly to get them to safety and then proceed to tell them (in no uncertain terms) that their behavior was not acceptable. As parents, we want our children to be happy and to feel good about themselves but more importantly, we want them to be safe. Kenny wants companies and employees to be happy and successful. He realizes, though, that they need to be protected from the destructive behaviors of bad managers.

If you are a business student, read this book and internalize its warnings so that you can someday help to bring about positive change for your employer. If you are a new manager, read this book so that you can be armed with the knowledge necessary to avoid some serious career pitfalls. If you are an employee, read this book and rest assured that you have the right to a certain level of reasonably fair treatment in the workplace. If you are a business owner or in upper management, read this book and remember that you set the tone and direction for your company, and if you tolerate (or worse yet, encourage) some of the behaviors and characteristics described in it, you are setting your company on a path to failure. If you are charged with the responsibility of leading or managing other people, in any capacity, you must read this book. And finally, if what you read offends you, do not dare to put the book down until you finish reading, and then change your behavior.

Richard Leake, Marketing Consultant

Introduction

We live in a business world that is becoming increasingly more competitive. Whether it is the cost associated with products or services or the style of personal attention that is given to the customer, businesses are always seeking an edge to remain a step ahead of the competition. Sadly, the intangible that is frequently neglected is the leadership aspect, which allows a company to prosper. Executives forget that an organization is only as good as the people who work there. They often disregard the need to place people into positions that match their talent and overlook someone who may be a great fit simply because the person is unappreciated by the abysmal managers they currently answer to. These are the people who have stimulated the reason for writing this book and they are the *Bastards* we talk about when we go home at night or when speaking with our colleagues.

Exceptional leadership is a much-needed component that has the power to guarantee business success, consumer fulfillment, and employee allegiance. To ensure these main beliefs, corporations often educate their managers about how to enhance and supervise employees. A distinct management approach is not the pre-eminent style when dealing with today's multicultural, multigenerational workplace. Today, there are more people looking for work, and the work force is getting older. It is very important to acknowledge that generational differences also play a role in how managers process topics such as incentive, authority, and compensation. A manager who makes the most of a range of leadership approaches will be more capable of dealing with would-be conflicts as well as suitably supervising those they manage.

Without the appropriate individuals in place, it does not matter what the forethought is for your business; accomplishment will be difficult to come by. To ease these and other burdens your business might face, I will discuss, in a straightforward manner, several issues that could make you a miserable supervisor. I don't expect many to take kindly to the approach, nor will I try to sugar-coat the issue. If the things discussed cause you to become irritated or angry, then maybe it is hitting close to home. If it doesn't bother you, then it's possible you are doing the right thing.

I have worked in businesses that had terrific culture and others that were run by people described throughout this book. As I worked, I also paid attention to the various qualities and mannerisms of not only those who were placed in charge, but also those who had the makings to be influential and showed promise to thrive in business. Regardless of how much education or experience you have, you can always learn if you are open-minded enough to listen. I've been a union representative, company manager, business owner, and teacher, and throughout my career, I always took time to ask questions of those considered by many to be inferior. The lowest person on the totem pole can contribute greatly to the success of an organization if you take the time to listen. Oftentimes they are in position to see and hear things that managers may fail to notice. My experience has led me to consider their opinions, and it is my hope that you will take my advice and do the same.

If you do, you may be able to extract information and refine areas that are a weakness. We can all improve. Use this reference as a light-hearted but piercing tool to help you become a better supervisor. After all, for some of you, someone did think little enough about you to give you a copy of this book, and for the rest, someone thought enough about you to want to see you succeed beyond measure. It's your choice.

Chapter 1
You Are a Tool

The resentment that criticism engenders can demoralize employees, family members, and friends, and still not correct the situation that has been condemned.

Dale Carnegie

Let me start by pointing out something that many managers take for granted: your employees are the people who will make or break you. It is their efforts that will make you look good or bad. Of course, if you are an arrogant supervisor who thinks the sun was created to rise and set in your ass, you will take the credit and claim that your ability to motivate (we'll talk about that later) is the reason your department did so well, but you need to remember this key point: you did not do it alone. Do you know why so there is such a high turnover rate in jobs that pay well? It's because the employees would rather earn less money and work for someone who values their effort than work for someone who is full of conceit, assumes the position he or she holds automatically warrants respect, and fails to exercise good judgment. Reverence is something that is earned; you can't make it a stipulation. If you believe you can, then you are a schmuck.

As an HR consultant, I have learned that many managers do not want me to tell them how they can be better. To the contrary; they would rather hear me say that the employees are the problem and help them understand that it is they who must change. I understand that it is difficult to measure the significance of the contribution of the HR element, but you should remember how you felt coming up the ladder yourself. How to substantiate what your employees do is no easy task, but all the same, educating others in regard to their effort will allow higher-ups within the organization to learn and understand how they contribute to the company's overall success.

All of this should go without saying, but too often there is so much effort placed on the numbers that managers are afraid to defend the work ethic of their employees. You would garner much esteem from your employees if you put aside *your* fear or insecurity and stick up for them once in a while. One of your primary responsibilities, as a manager, is to make sure that others view your workers as an indispensable part of the organization, while you take upon yourself the role of being a sounding board to their needs. Doing so may help them be more productive and also help you, since their performance affects the way you are perceived as a manager. Why should someone else evaluate your staff and point out the efforts they are making? When you accept the position of manager, you automatically become an extension of the HR division. It is in your best interest to learn as much as you can about this complicated and multifaceted business task.

Care should be taken to not form an opinion about the HR element until you fully understand exactly what they do. Many managers have not even done the very job for which they are cracking the whip to try and get results, nor do they appreciate the value of understanding human behavior. The significance of being able to train and encourage employees, and point them in the right direction, is lost in the irony that most managers haven't even been trained themselves to handle the new responsibility that comes with their leadership position. What is even sadder is that when the employees try to provide input, so they can obtain the resources they need to be successful from management, they are told to simply shut up and do their jobs.

If you are a manager who thinks you have all the answers, you're an idiot. If you truly knew it all, you wouldn't be having any problems, would you? I remember one supervisor, who would typically remain notably quiet throughout meetings, who was asked why he didn't speak up more often. We should all keep his response in mind: "I'm already aware of what I know, and it does not impress anyone for me to spout off about it. I'm more interested in learning what I don't know, and the people who are providing that information help me with that. I learn more by listening." This statement should be like a stake in the heart to all you vampire-type managers who simply want to suck the life out of those who work for you, who do not want to appear *less knowledgeable* than those you supervise. It's an atrocious business attitude to own, and you should do your best to rid yourself of this personal development barrier! Hopefully, what you learn from reading this book will help you change the negative approach you have toward your workforce.

Your prideful mind-set doesn't impress anyone, and you should know that, more often than not, it's a predecessor to a fall. Your employees understand that you may have more knowledge regarding the inner workings of your organization than they do; however, it is also likely that you can learn from them as well. Before you think this is simply manager bashing, please understand that I also acknowledge that you may often come across employees who simply do not have the necessary tools to be successful. They may not have the drive, basic skill set, or learning capability, which will ultimately create problems that you simply cannot resolve. In cases such as these, it is important to cut your losses and find someone who can contribute to the organization in a positive manner. Care should be taken so as to not come across as arrogant in order to sidestep the impression that you are biased toward this group. An overly self-important attitude could lead to damaging outcomes in a labor relations type of inquest.

For the most part, however, it is imperative that employers see that human resource units become more involved in designing, not just executing, a company's strategic plan. This approach creates a team atmosphere and allows those employees who seem insignificant, in your eyes, to strive to be better and learn more so they may contribute to organizational success. Many of your employees know what kind of performance is needed as well as the customer or production issues that serve as barriers to their success. It is not an admission of incompetence for you to ask them for their opinion once in a while.

In fact, this approach could actually help to generate better relations with your staff; it could also improve your unit's productivity. Think about the benefit this could have in a union environment, as you cultivate more harmony in the midst of often difficult relations or as you recognize the competencies that others have, which can serve to your advantage.

There are many opinions as to the most important role of HR professionals. Many businesses allow division managers to do the hiring for their units. This has a terrific upside, since those managers usually know what they need from a new hire to make their area profitable, but they may choose new hires based on the wrong factors. For example, a hiring manager may look for someone who does not pose a knowledge threat or may have a weaker personality. What you end up with is an employee that is not skilled enough to recognize that the problem isn't their inability to do the job; it's the piss ant supervisor who doesn't want to feel threatened by someone that may be able to offer helpful suggestions. Personally speaking, my belief is that HR's greatest contribution to a company is the ability to acquire and retain leading talent. Many hiring managers are not trained in the HR area, which leads to other problems.

As a manager, you play a vital part in devising a strategy that draws the brightest and most promising employees as well as creating plans that keep current talent on your roster. Training and development systems keep current employees motivated with the understanding they have opportunity to flourish in a company that takes interest in their professional growth. But a question surfaces in organizations that allow lousy, lazy managers to show favoritism, misuse systems that are designed to provide quality customer prospects to each employee, or place unrealistic demands on employees when common sense should prevail. Are these managers so afraid of appearing inept that they refuse to make a truly clever decision? Here is a piece of philosophical meat you can chew on that will almost certainly bring about a brief disruption in your logic: failing is simply a means to discover how *not* to do something. Although there may be some disappointment associated with it, if you fail forward, then you can become better yourself.

Nobody is perfect (not even you), so it is not realistic to expect your employees to be. For this reason, you can be more helpful by taking advice from others with more experience than you have. If you actually value the opinions of members of your workforce, you may possibly learn together and your turnover rates will drop off. Imagine how refreshing the atmosphere would be to go to work and have employees who respect you because you have taken steps to make them feel appreciated and respected.

Adequate hiring practices are also a cost-saving measure. You must realize the workforce demographics you have to work with, the competition in your region, skills needed to be successful in various positions, and whether you possess the tools to facilitate learning in the workplace once someone is hired. The only yardstick you will have to monitor the results of your hiring risk (and it is always a risk) is the net revenue obtained by the business. If you are an employer who believes in frequent turnover and views the human element as being expendable, then most likely you are also a company that is continuously training new employees. Furthermore, your business probably has lower net revenue due to increased overtime, which results from the wait period until a former employee is replaced, lower quality due to the fatigue of overworked employees, and the time it takes for new employees to get up to speed.

If you are a business owner or leader in an organization, I recommend you take a closer look at the useless manager you have entrusted to care for your company; such managers keep organizations from achieving their sales or revenue goals because they are afraid of being overshadowed by their workers. Those managers think their workers are insignificant, but they do not realize they need those people to come through for them in order to meet those goals. Internal programs that enhance employee education needs produce a workforce that is happy and willing to help the organization achieve success because of the pride they take in their job and the company. You, Mr. or Ms. Manager, are not the engine that makes the wheels turn; you're just the driver; you may need a refresher course. Your employees should be considered your top customer groups as you develop your business.[1]

1   Wright, P.M., Snell, S.A., McMahan, G.C., & Gerhart, B. "Comparing Line and HR Executives' Perceptions of HR Effectiveness: Services, Roles, and Contributions." *Human Resource Management*, 2001, 111-123.

Most companies that hope to be successful do their best to seek out and hold on to their most cherished customer group – their employees. In our ultra competitive business environment this is becoming a more competitive task that occurs more often than in the past. The capacity to demonstrate their professional gifts is something most employees look forward to doing. By allowing, or enabling, them to showcase their competitive aptitudes, a business enhances this oft overlooked customer segment as the battle is stepped up to keep top talent. Instead of being threatened by them, embrace what they bring to the table and allow them to make you look good as well.

Chapter 2
You Need a Bully Beat Down

The way you see them is the way you treat them, and the way you treat them is the way they often become.

Zig Ziglar

By now you probably realize that I am singling poor managers out as the problem in the workplace, *not* employees. If it isn't clear to you yet, let's go a step further and determine if you are a workplace bully. There are probably a few people reading this that will puff their chests out with pride and argue they have the right to say what they please, but they should just shut up. No one has the right to treat others as though they are expendable, irrelevant, or worthless. If you have people like that working for you, then obviously you are a useless manager since you did not make an appropriate hire or train people appropriately. If you would rather jeopardize your business so you can belittle your employees, then go and sing your own praises to your friends at the bar and brag about how you maltreated someone. FYI, they're probably calling you a dumb-ass when you leave, so don't be too delighted with yourself.

Precisely what is workplace bullying? Persecution or bullying on the job takes many forms, such as unwanted physical demonstrations, but it is more than that. As a result, the definition isn't so easy to communicate; it could materialize in these behaviors:

7

- ✓ Name-calling
- ✓ Gossip/rumors (supervisors would *never* do that, would they?)
- ✓ Coercion
- ✓ Degradation/humiliation
- ✓ Threats (what a great motivational technique!)
- ✓ Criticism
- ✓ Provocative teasing
- ✓ Spying (such as when you have a workplace pet gather intel for you; it's a terrific way to destroy morale)
- ✓ Needlessly shadowing
- ✓ Withholding information that could help employees be more productive
- ✓ Insistent denigration

It is normally frowned upon for employees to engage in relationships with their supervisors, for obvious reasons (I'm going to assume the majority of you have common sense here, although if these things pertain to you, most likely you don't), but people are human, and they do make mistakes. These mistakes can be very detrimental to a business, since the appearance of favoritism can rapidly establish itself into a situation. Even if you are the lousy supervisor depicted in this book, put yourself in the shoes of another for a moment as I describe the following scenario an employee may be struggling with:

You are aware of a circumstance of a sexual nature that occurred involving one of your coworkers and your supervisor. Even while you do your job to the best of your ability and habitually meet company goals, you feel as though there is a special preference given to your coworker, who regularly underachieves. As you continue to try and improve yourself, you are repeatedly slighted when you offer suggestions about how your unit can improve performance. One day, during a meeting, you are verbally condemned by the same coworker. As you defend yourself, you are rebuked for doing so by the same supervisor, who gives you a reprimand that is placed in your personnel file; all the while, your coworker is overlooked as being the agitator or primary contributor to the confrontation. The coworker doesn't get a slap on the wrist and is eventually promoted.

Within the legal community, the person who is generally considered at fault in the commission of a violent crime is known as the primary physical aggressor. In other words, if the person who claims they were assaulted points to their fat lip as evidence, it doesn't mean another person will be arrested or charged. The point is that what may appear to be accurate may, in reality, be reflective of a bigger issue. Starry-eyed relations within the workplace are capable of leading to serious consequences. Allegations of poor judgment, ethics violations, preferential treatment, reductions in productivity, and employee emotional states that result in a diminution of their perceived value are factors that should be considered when thinking of engaging in this type of activity but is usually overlooked due to selfish urges on the part of the active participants. Usually, the notion that the behavior described may possibly lead to a claim of sexual harassment rarely enters the mind of those involved. The business situation described is a version of this scenario, and my point is that common sense should overcome the errors of a bullying supervisor who may choose to ignore the cause of an action based on personal relationships.

How would this type of workplace situation make *you* feel? If you find that this state of affairs would be inappropriate if it happened to you, then what would make it proper to tolerate another person being subjected to the same treatment? The answer *should* be exceedingly straightforward—*nothing*! There is nothing about this incident that would warrant you, or anyone else, being exposed to this type of workplace bullying, because that is exactly what it is, it just doesn't get recognized in that context. Think about the repercussions associated with the bullying or disparaging treatment your employees are forced to deal with. Maltreatment often results in the person who is being targeted suffering psychological and physical problems. If you do not believe it has an impact on the organization, consider the monetary loss caused by a reduction in productivity or repeated turnover. The company may lose a true superstar employee simply because of a piss-poor supervisor that has no idea about how to interact with diverse personalities in the workplace.

Bear in mind how often we read about a worker who was

mistreated going back to their workplace and resorting to violence against coworkers as well as themselves. Although these events are a small percentage in comparison to the number of *unreported* incidents, victims of bullying typically feel defenseless, lonely, aggravated, discouraged, and upset. These emotions produce stress-related illnesses and other ailments. A person's family and personal friendships may also be influenced negatively, which generates even more bitterness directed toward you and stress for your employee. Is this the kind of employee you really want to spawn? Doesn't it make more sense, and isn't it better for the profitability and success of your business, to develop each person by using the special talent that each person possesses?

Get over yourself; your employees are not a threat to you if they are happy and productive; they are going to make you look good, which is a feather in your cap to those you report to. Success is a team effort, unless you are playing darts, so start focusing on generating a team atmosphere.

Every workplace has a unique culture of its own. Some people fit in well, while others may struggle to assimilate. A good manager will make that adaptation easier if they take the time to become acquainted with each person's particular talents. Managers who are successful ensure that an employee's responsibilities match their abilities and enable them to excel. A good manager is *not* an oppressive authoritarian who practices self-indulgency while quashing the confidence and drive of those who look to them for support. If your organization is failing, your point of view has created the environment that you see every day. If you believe that you have to do it all because nobody else is as good as you are, your workplace probably reflects that attitude. Stop acting like a puffed-up jerk and change yourself. If you do, you may find yourself on the receiving end of something satisfactory.

Chapter 3
Don't Treat Employees Like Children

Some of us will do our jobs well and some will not, but we will be judged by only one thing: the result.

Vince Lombardi

You may disagree with this section, because you may believe it is essential to treat your employees like children. Your style may be to say, "If you make enough calls and schedule enough appointments, I will buy you lunch," or "If you get enough of your appointments to show up, I will let you have Saturday off so you can spend time with your family," and so on. Why don't you throw a lollipop in there as well? While much of this section reverts back to the chapter on motivation, it needs to be pointed out that employees want to be treated with respect, and believe it or not, they want to succeed. They take great offense, as would you, to being treated like a child while carrying out their daily activities.

There are always going to be some people who need to be more closely monitored, but usually, these types are few and far between. What we are talking about here is the manager who doesn't distinguish between the habitually poor performer and everyone else who constantly strives to reach their target objectives. Often this stems from the friendships that are developed between an employee and the employer. So what do you do when a situation surfaces? You cover yourself by making some indiscriminate threat to everyone instead of dealing with the root of the problem. I'm willing to bet that many of you have offended an entire group by taking some form of blanket action instead of confronting your workplace "pet." An all-inclusive e-mail or memo or a public tirade could produce resentment toward you or toward the one who is responsible for the problem. The real source of an issue may not even be the "teacher's pet," but you, as the supervisor, are just too pusillanimous (look it up, or you can just use the shorter version) to deal with an issue head on. If there is a concern over an employee's behavior, uses of company time, or their manner of dress, have a conversation with that person separately. You are also being paid to do a job, and your failure to treat the root of an issue only creates more acrimony toward you when one and all are held responsible.

Are you guilty of frequently talking on your cell phone or texting your spouse, significant other, or anyone else? I'm sure it's important to *you* to keep your family or household managed while you are at work. So here's a question: why do you chastise your workforce for doing the same? You know that your employees also have lives outside of work, and they have the same concerns you do. Even though there is no justification for someone taking advantage of the company and the time they are meant to be working, is it really that bad for them to take, or make, a call to check up on their family? This is definitely not a situation that classifies as cheating the employer. If you want to point fingers, point them at the people who take smoke breaks every fifteen minutes or visit your office to discuss a television show you each watched the night before.

While you are yelling at someone who gets out of their chair to move around and stretch their legs or rest their eyes from the constant haze of the computer screen for a few minutes, think about the others who are persistently disappearing for extended periods of time. This is one of the reasons that employees need to be dealt with as individuals, not as a group. I don't smoke; I don't get out of my chair and wander around the halls; and I don't take any breaks until I have completed my tasks, so don't come in and tell *us* that *we* need to do our jobs. It's not *us* that are taking advantage of your (cough, cough, cough) good nature. Just in case you have never thought about how to effectively deal with your employees, here is a simple strategy spelled out for your immediate consideration (because you don't have much time to lose):

✓ Deal with people exclusively
✓ Assign punishment individually (unless it's a group problem)
✓ Understand that employees have lives away from the office
✓ Treat employees as adults
✓ And finally, bear in mind the Golden Rule: Offer your employees the same level of respect and decorum that you want to be bestowed to you.

As a supervisor, you need to have a clear plan of how you will deal with situations that arise. Many successful athletes visualize an event prior to actually performing it. They often rehearse in their own minds how they move in relation to their opponent or see themselves moving about in explicit detail. It's just another way they prepare for that one moment in time that may possibly separate them from those who didn't ready themselves completely. So let me remind you of something: if you don't know where you are going, then any road will get you there. You need to prepare; you should think about the scenarios that may come up and then consider what you will do to rectify them. Many companies use a policy and procedure manual to help you, but you must remember that these are merely guidebooks to help you reach the desired destination. Think of them as road maps to help you find your way, but also spend time visualizing how you would act, or react, to situations. I'm sure most of you watch television, so while you are watching programs like *Mad Men*, *The Office*, or *The Apprentice*, think about how you would, or should, handle situations that come up during those shows. There is no reason you can't learn while you are being entertained. Learning should always be a part of your personal self-help catalog.

From top to bottom, supervisors and executives alike simply do not realize the value of planning. To the contrary, they indiscriminately jump in and embark on their vengeful mission in an illogical manner that could eventually bring about negative results. It makes sense to use a logical approach to solving workplace dilemmas, although incompetent managers are deficient in planning wisdom; they cannot correct a business ship traveling a potentially destructive course. The role of a leader ought to be to cultivate confidence, teamwork, and an environment that bequeaths cooperation among all members of the organization, not just those in your unit. If you don't realize this, then you probably have (or will have) some big problems at work.

You should also remember this key point: people and their situations are not always an entirely comprehensible issue. Situations are not always what they appear, so you must take time to ascertain all the facts before deciding who is right and who is wrong. One of your goals should be taking the time to grasp an issue before you ask for understanding of it. This does several things. First, it allows you to empathize with the person you are dealing with. In turn, you show that you are considering the entirety of the issue. Second, you reveal to the person(s) involved that you want to hear their side of the story. Listening is a key attribute to being a good leader and will help you make a completely informed decision. And third, this approach helps you be more decisive, made because you have taken the time to consider each and every facet of the issue. More than anything else, conducting yourself in this manner will help boost you into the category of leader, not just a manager, which is the intention of this entire book.

Having the capability to get things done is one of the primary traits of a good supervisor. But getting things done doesn't mean using your authority to abuse those who work for you by barking orders or irrationally hounding them based on your emotional state. To the contrary, you must be able to set your feelings aside long enough to get others to connect with you so a goal can be successfully achieved. Managers who are able to treat others the way they want to be treated bring about the desired result and are keepers in the eyes of upper management. Although it can be difficult at times, it is an indispensable attribute for you to remain unruffled in the face of problems that frequently occur. Having the ability to handle these issues and treat your people with respect will almost surely reduce the occurrence of these irritations.

Supervisors who behave toward their staff as though they are made up of adolescents will rapidly find out that it is just not practical to draw attention to employee errors. People who make mistakes or do not produce as you would like may not be pleased by the outcome of their conduct, but they usually behave with good intentions. The area that isn't clear to them is the outcome correlation.

As a manager, one of your functions is to help workers see how their actions may have created a predicament, but you have to do it without treating them like children. Isn't the goal to have them make better choices? It may sound a lot like raising a child, but would you really slap your child for spilling a glass of water? I *hope* not! By calming down and permitting yourself to control your thoughts sensibly, you can handle situations more effectively. Try taking a nonjudgmental approach and broach minor issues in a roundabout way. Ask a simple question such as, "What happened?" This may show them that their conduct may have been a factor. This may also permit each of you to arrive at a solution to the problem, which places the onus on the employee; they now understand that a repeat occurrence is a breach of the solution they helped to come up with.

Intermittently, a blunder might cause a more serious business dilemma. You may become angry if the issue could have been easily avoided, so be certain the circumstances do not develop into an unwarranted personal attack on the worker who is to blame. Communicate your dissatisfaction with the occurrence, not the person. Also, employees may direct anger toward you, but you must keep your cool and reply in a more professional demeanor, since people have a tendency to react in kind. Your reaction can easily diffuse (or escalate) a situation, so think before you speak.

To wrap this up, top managers are able to mix optimistic enthusiasm with purposeful and focused assessments, so that productivity is drummed up and turmoil is kept to a minimum. This is an effective performance management trick that demonstrates that you can skillfully shed light on priorities and make sure they are adhered to. Just as the Vince Lombardi quote implies, it is up to you how you will be judged.

Chapter 4
You Couldn't Lead a Horse to Water

You do not lead by hitting people over the head—that's assault, not leadership.

Dwight D. Eisenhower

Our culture is vastly different from those in South Korea, Thailand, or Taiwan, in that we place great importance on external rewards for our efforts. The regions mentioned look at built-in incentives such as praise or admiration from their superiors more so than monetary motivation. That doesn't do us much good, though, since we are simply playing with the cards we have been dealt. The biggest question is how we handle our business.

With motivation being our concern at this point, we should recognize self-motivation is the best way to increase someone's effectiveness. There are hundreds of motivational techniques that can be used to stimulate employees. Discussing each would be an act of futility since each individual responds differently to various stimuli, and most likely, since you are reading this book, you haven't taken the time to even consider ways to encourage them. You may also turn a blind eye to these ideas if you are a pig-headed fool who only cares about yourself. The trick is to discover what each individual reacts to in the most advantageous manner for your company.

As I said, there are a number of ways to motivate others, but the trick is to find out what each person is motivated by. Motivations can be based on the need for safety, shelter, or security; based on people's thoughts, values, and feelings; or based on the behavior of others in relation to their personal desires. I don't want to get too involved in psychoanalytical discussions, but these are referred to as need-based, cognitive, and noncognitive motivations.

If you supervise a large number of employees, you need a solid understanding of leadership before you try to motivate them, because sure as the sun rises in the morning, you are bound to screw it up if you think you're a leader simply because of your title. There are numerous people who will offer advice about leadership, so I'll provide my two cents' worth also (although I think it's worth quite a bit more). You first need to decide if you are going to be a proactive or reactive person in charge. You first need to realize that a proactive approach is better than a reactive one. A reactive person allows events to control them. Often, this emotional response forces you to do or say things you later wish you could take back. Sadly enough, once your words hit the air, there is no taking them back. You can always apologize, but for the most part, the damage has already been done. People are often hurt more by words than by any amount of physical actions. Bruises go away, the emotional scars you leave due to a negative comment.

On the other hand, proactive managers do their best to control the outcome by thinking ahead. It is easy to imagine scenarios and then consider what you may do or say. That type of visualization is a form of proactive attachment. Planning ahead and considering outcomes before something actually transpires is a fantastic way to improve your managerial skills and sets you on the right path to becoming a more capable leader. Being proactive also means you are slower to anger. Anger can induce you to take wrongful action.

A thorough understanding about what can be expected from your employees should be considered before taking on a certain approach. Your line of attack may produce some passive resistance to your efforts. You will know this is occurring when you witness work slowdowns, unintentional (but possibly planned) errors, or employees not doing anything more than they are asked to do. You won't find many going above and beyond what is expected of them.

Your workforce may become apathetic or indifferent; they may simply come to work to get a paycheck. They do not have any desire to do more and could care less about what happens. Many probably already see the writing on the wall and are just waiting for the axe to fall (either on you or on themselves). What you say is probably the equivalent of nails being dragged across a chalkboard. They may be obedient (especially if you bullied them into compliance), but they are just going through the motions. Their attitude is, "Who the hell cares?"

This book will help you learn how to get them to buy into agreement, engagement, and passion. These three things can turn your fruitless office into a dynamic, revenue-generating machine. Those who are in agreement with you may not have the energy to go all out for you. You need to take them to the next level, which is engagement.

Employees who are engaged are not only in harmony with your ways but also want to be involved. These people are your eager beavers who strive to find ways to do more and apply themselves by making an additional effort. You may think that this is the best you can do as far as motivation, but there is one more level you can muster from someone.

Make them passionate about their job! This may not be the healthiest way to live one's life, but these employees put their work above everything else. Pursuing professional development, climbing the corporate ladder, and having few secondary interests outside of their job is a characteristic of this person. This type of obsessed, often fixated, and possibly overanxious employee can be a great tool for helping you reach deadlines, but use care; there are some serious negatives if they cannot find balance. Try to attain a balance of enthusiasm and passion if you can. This is where you need to be tuned in to those working for you.

If you take some time to reflect about or silently observe the people in your office, you should be able to pick which ones fit into the assorted categories. I'm also willing to bet that you will be able to see how effective, or unsuccessful, you have been by studying these people. Remember that the culture of your organization is a reflection of your leadership. Do not call them to your office and chastise them if they are not where you want them to be. This section is about helping you find a way to make them want to change for the good of the business and for their own well-being.

I've used the terms "managers" and "leaders" throughout this book, but until now, we have not really delved into the leadership role thoroughly. Just because you hold the title "manager" does not mean you are a leader. But before we begin discussing the difference between leaders and managers, it is important to understand what leadership is. Most successful sports teams have at least one player who is the leader. Within the military setting, leaders prove themselves to be adaptable, courageous, and knowledgeable. History is filled with examples of great political leaders who have changed the course of events, but what do they have in common?

Leadership can be defined as a method of motivating others to get things done. Just as professional athletes, military leaders, and politicians use their position to attain particular objectives, business professionals are also capable of conducting themselves in a way that motivates subordinates to want to follow their lead.

Conversely, leadership is not a trait that everyone possesses. Some people are satisfied being followers and do not want the responsibility of making tough decisions. I'm sure that if you think about it honestly, this may apply to you as well. Responsibility is a key component to being a truly effective leader, and even if you are a responsible individual, you may not have the flair to assume a leading role.

Leaders are the people that others look at to get the job done. They are the people who are counted on to set the example for others. A leader can be defined as someone who does not say anything that would be considered wrong by a subordinate, and if they do, they are willing to listen to opposing points of view. They do not ask anyone to do anything that they would be unwilling to do themselves, and they do not belittle any member of their staff. Leaders realize that each person within the organization contributes to the organization's success, regardless of how trivial that person thinks their job is. Leaders motivate others to strive to be the best at what they do and to take pride in knowing that the tasks they perform help the overall mission of the company. Ralph Waldo Emerson once said, "Who you are speaks so loudly I can't hear what you're saying[2]." What this means, in the context it is being applied, is that your actions will speak louder than your words. People are inspired by what they see in those they look up to – not by what they hear which, many times, is hypocritical when compared to a person's actions.

The most effectual leaders strive to persistently seek information from company management and share it with their subordinates. I know some of you don't deserve the position you have, so let me make the last sentence more comprehensible for you: *good managers* who are accomplished at their job take the initiative to ask questions of *their* supervisors so they can make the business more successful (and allow their employees to be successful as well). If you refuse to ask questions simply because you are afraid the answer will be no, you are a total hypocrite if you tell your employees they shouldn't take no for an answer.

Have you ever told an employee to be assertive when they make their sales calls? What would you do if they came to you and said, "I didn't want to call because I was afraid the person would tell me no?" Why do you feel it's okay for you to use that as an excuse to not ask questions from upper management? I'll give you the answer: it's simply because you are a fraud. You preach self-confidence and assurance, and you should, but your actions make it obvious that you don't exercise the same conviction yourself.

Corporations are in business to be successful, and if you do not provide upper-level executives the data they need to modify their approach to a particular area, you are failing as a team player. They need to know what your sales staff is doing to meet their sales objectives, and they depend on your input to help your staff be more productive. This is simply a good way of doing business, since it makes sense to understand the various demographics of each sales district. The manager who is afraid to perform market research, is shy about offering the data to the corporate office, or merely defers to what has been done for years is doing the company a disservice. No good comes by failing to show some initiative and provide opinions that may result in increased revenue if the initiative were taken.

---

2   Emerson, Ralph W. "Quotes Museum." 2010. http://www.quotes-museum. com/quote/28412 (accessed January 2, 2011).

Generals acquire battlefield data from those in the trenches so they can make modifications to the battle plan; the same goes for business leaders. They rely on those placed in positions of authority to provide enough information so they can alter marketing materials or amend business plans to reach the target audience. You do not deserve your position if you do not take action to allow your people to be successful.

To fulfill the obligations of your position, you may need to make choices that impinge on the natural order. The choices you make and the information you provide have an effect on other people's lives, so you need to stop being afraid of taking more of a leadership role. You must begin by facing your own limitations and admitting that you don't know it all; it is perfectly acceptable to ask for help. This can be difficult, but if you want to be a leader, you have to confront unpleasant circumstances and decide how much energy you will put in to help your business improve. Leadership involves several intangibles, such as wisdom, technological competence, and cultural awareness; however, the prevalent intangible is the ability to persuade others. This does not mean that you have to be a tyrant, though. Being in a position of authority often compels some to believe they are entitled to admiration and reverence, which leads them to becoming complacent and refusing to heed (or even ask for) the suggestions of others.

To quote F. Scott Fitzgerald, "The test of a first-rate intelligence is the ability to hold two opposed ideas in mind at the same time and still retain the ability to function.[3]" The biggest problem of worthless managers is they are not capable of holding two opposing ideas in mind. They simply don't want to take advice from anyone else, so they close their minds to the fact that others may have something constructive to offer, because to them, that is a threat. Talking to your workforce to unmask what works and what does not is a good leadership practice. You need to remain open-minded about the information you acquire; effectual leaders do *not* take what they learn personally, since the data collected can help rectify oversights and breakdowns that are occurring. You must be confident in your

3   Fitzgerald, F Scott. "The Crack Up." 1936. http://www.quotationspage.com/quote/90.html (accessed December 3, 2010).

own abilities and not be afraid to make decisions that challenge the status quo. If you do not performing as a manager in a manner that garners loyalty and respect, then those working for you will not feel compelled to do their best either.

Another quality that outstanding managers have is that they are able to guide those who work for them and persuade their subordinates to stick to the rules.[4] This can be a tricky part of management; some managers become friendly with their staff and are not able to shift from the role of friend to the job of supervisor. When this happens, productivity tends to decline, and those who are not part of the clique feel left out. Managers can have a difficult time recovering from this, because they then have to choose between their friends, who are not performing up to task, and workers who are not part of the clique but execute their tasks properly.

I've been a victim of this last situation, as many of you have too, and it is simply an understatement to say you are a total jerk if you allow this to go on. I'd even be willing to say that your business is suffering thanks to this type of mind-set on your part. If the decision is hard for you, then let me simplify it: get your head out of your buddy's ass (or get theirs out of yours) and do the job the way it is supposed to be done. If you can't do that, then eventually you will be the one worrying about the door hitting you in the rear end on your way out, because in time, what goes around comes around. You can only place the blame on others for so long before the magnifying glass eventually gets turned onto you.

Here are a few leadership traits that will help you become better if you develop them. Leaders are those who:
- ✓ Lead
- ✓ Have followers
- ✓ Seek change
- ✓ Are proactive
- ✓ Take risks
- ✓ Look for what is right
- ✓ Have charisma

In contrast, managers are those who:

---

4   Clark, Donald. "Concepts of Leadership." 2008. www.nwlink. com/~donclark/leader/leadcon.html (accessed June 9, 2010).

- ✓ Manage
- ✓ Have subordinates
- ✓ Look for stability
- ✓ Are reactive
- ✓ Reduce risk
- ✓ Endeavor to be right
- ✓ Hold proper authority

As you look at the differences, it is apparent that the best leaders possess all the traits shown, but those who are destined to remain managers do not possess the traits associated with a leader. Also, a bad manager may not even be capable of doing the things on that list effectively.

Leadership is not a trait that everyone possesses. There is an overwhelming dissimilarity involving leaders and managers. *A superior manager does things right, whereas a superior leader does the right thing,* assuming the right thing requires a purpose, a course, an intention, a dream, a hope, a line of attack, a direction, and a means to accomplish it.[5] If you are going to try and be a leader who uses your clout to get things done, then you should probably expect substandard results. On the other hand, if your intent is to garner respect; stimulate others in a positive manner; turn out employees who are in agreement with you, engaged, and passionate about their work; and be a true business partner who enthusiastically wants to be a success, then you will pay attention to the words of Dwight D. Eisenhower quoted at the beginning of this chapter.

---

5   Schruijer, S. and Vansina, L. "Leadership and Organization Change: An Introduction." *European Journal of Work & Organizational Psychology* (1999).

Chapter 5
You Spend Too Much Time Stimulating Yourself

A team that has character doesn't need stimulation.

Tom Laundry

Now that we have discussed leadership, let's talk about what actually motivates people. This is the one subject that invariably creates the biggest problem for the abysmal manager. Just as the chapter title says, you spend entirely too much time stimulating yourself. The "what's in it for me?" attitude lends considerably to the problem that is formed in your ineffectual psyche as you constantly place yourself first and the customer or employee second; the problem is exacerbated when you ignore others to be an advocate for yourself. Generating a culture of distinction in a workplace involves more than simply practicing good management principles and applying sound leadership. It is about instilling in employees the need to focus on the one tangible asset that can make or break the organization: the customer.

Many of you are so caught up in how others see you that you forget that your arrogance is hurting your ability to become a better manager or develop into a true leader. You are your own worst enemy in this regard, and your narcissistic actions lead you to search for compliments and admiration to fuel your insecurity. When you see yourself as being omnipotent, unmatched, and a cut above everyone else, you forget that success in business involves a number of people. I'm willing to bet that you often say that you have to "do it all" or "you wear many hats because others can't seem to get the job done," fueling your exaggerated self-image. This rant that you frequently go on, in all probability, avoids accepting blame and advances your own worth at the expense of those you are supposed to be leading.

Since I'm on a roll here, I don't want to stop this rebuke just yet (I hope this is making many of you squirm just knowing that someone placed this book on your desk because of this very chapter). Many of you only care about your own feelings and take full advantage of others to elevate yourself in some twisted manner. You probably make your employees work on weekends or holidays as a form of punishment, while you are nowhere to be found. Being insensitive to the needs of your employees is a simple indication that you lack the necessary traits to be a leader, and the person who promoted you ought to be placing a magnifying glass over you, like a kid does to an ant in the sunlight, for the simple reason that you are doing more harm to the business than any inferior product ever could.

If you keep an open mind and overlook your vanity for a few minutes, this section may be more beneficial to you than you realize. There is nothing wrong with having confidence in yourself; the problem comes when you refuse to examine the ideas of others and then revert to the notion that nobody is as good as you. You probably have some real talent, but you need to mature into a bona fide business leader. In all actuality, you are probably suffering more from insecurity, and you hide behind the vanity as a means to avoid being hurt. A person's psyche is full of defense mechanisms; insecurity may well manifest itself as an egocentric personality, which may be the opposite of who you really are. Yes, I am trying to give you that golden benefit of the doubt; the mind can, unquestionably, be very creative and turn us into somebody we really aren't.

But I am not writing a book to help you with your psychological issues, I simply want to provide you with a clear-cut, simple approach to help you be a better manager, so with all that in mind and in order to promote the mission of the company, those of you at the top must make clear directives and offer good advice so that each staff member understands the commitment that must be made to clients and consumers. As that happens, then a first-rate business reputation will emerge, and your self-righteous perception will be replaced with true admiration. This opinion of others then becomes an asset that will be part of the company and is the first step in a proactive plan.

We talked briefly about some of this before; it is important for you to understand where various motivations originate from; these concepts apply to your staff as well as yourself. Remember, you were once somebody who was coming up the ladder, and you may have had to put up with the big-headed despot I previously described. Motivation is no different for you than it is for those who work for you, and much analysis has been done in an effort to determine what it is that inspires people to want to succeed.

Psychologist Abraham Maslow focused much of his research on what motivated human beings. He categorized a ladder of needs based on two classifications: deficiency and growth needs. Maslow reasoned that everyone had to meet the need of a lower level before they could move to another level of growth.[6]

To start, let's discuss what a few of these identified needs are. Self-actualization is the ability to realize and help accomplish personal agendas, while esteem needs help people have a good opinion of themselves. It is a person's sense of belonging that encompasses this portion. Most people want approval and recognition of their talent or contributions as a means to justify their existence. This is a key in the workplace, as employees want to know their efforts are appreciated. Maslow believed that this need exists in everyone but is often thwarted by the environment.[7] Maslow's theory suggests that you should create an environment for your employee that is favorable to helping them achieve this pinnacle, and they will serve well in the future.

Social needs include the need to have friends, to give and receive love, and to feel that one belongs or fits in. Anything that correlates to associations with others denotes a relationship to social needs. As an example, new employees might need to be accepted by their new

6 Davis, Stephen F., and Palladino, Joseph J. *Psychology*. 5th ed. Upper Saddle River: Prentice Hall, 2009.
7 Davis, Stephen F., and Palladino, Joseph J. *Psychology*. 5th ed. Upper Saddle River: Prentice Hall, 2009.

coworkers. As a manager, it would be a good idea to help them get acquainted with others. If you have any extracurricular functions you do as a group, such as bowling night or a group outing, you should ask if they want to participate. Any shared events will help to inspire your employees and meet a need of belonging in a social setting. Still another way to establish how an employee feels is to take an attitude survey. Attitude surveys seek input from employees to determine their feeling about such topics such as the work they perform, their supervisor, the work environment, training and development opportunities, and the firm's compensation system. This approach shows your concern for those under your watch and helps you to meet one of the more important needs: the need to fit in.

Safety needs can be met by living in family-friendly areas, having adequate insurance and financial stability, and feeling confident about retaining one's job. Nobody likes to feel threatened, either physically or emotionally. Many of us worry about our own personal safety or the safety of loved ones. How we meet that need is another matter, however. For some, it means living in an area that is considered safe and free from the threat of crime, while for others, it might simply mean having health insurance. Job security is always an issue, as is being able to financially support one's family.

Maslow observed that if a person felt they were in harm's way, then higher needs would not be given a great deal of consideration. If you ever felt threatened in some way, you probably did not put any thought into your self-esteem, love interests, sexual needs, or self-actualization. The controlling factor was fear, fear of what was going to happen at that moment to you or someone else. If one of your employees feels threatened, they will not be able to concentrate on the task at hand. You have to shift much of your focus on that person to ensure that work-related tasks are being met so the business will not suffer.

Finally, physiological needs are those basic requirements needed in order to survive and function normally, such as food, water, air, and rest. I want to discuss Maslow's ideas in detail because it is crucial that you, as an emerging leader, realize how they affect the workplace and how you can be a better manager by simply understanding their effects on employees. As you continue to read through this section, you may realize you have an overriding need that falls into these categories as well. If you fail to acknowledge that your employees seek fulfillment of basic needs in the workplace, or if you realize it but do not try to meet those needs, you are more of an ass than I've depicted already.

This next area is one that often gets cited as a genuine employee criticism; when you ask a staff member when they hear from their boss, they usually answer, "When I do something wrong, or when they think I did something wrong." Because of this viewpoint, performance evaluations can be stressful. They may look at it as a time when their shortcomings are highlighted, with little or no attention paid to their strengths. This practice can become so stressful that an employee may just move on to another company, which could harm your organization. While the top performers get most of the positive attention, it's the second teamers that keep things working. An old Moor proverb states, "Choose your companions before you choose your road." For the most part, you've already chosen your companions (employees); now you must choose the road you are going to take, to motivate them to be more dedicated to the business, which will also make them want to improve their performance and grow professionally.

Remarkable things can happen in your business if you know how to bring out the best in others. Everyone has a talent, and if you can find each employee's talent and develop it, that is a recipe for success. If one employee appears to be favored by the supervisors, a hostile atmosphere could develop, and employees may turn against each other.

Motivation more often than not comes back to a simple question: "What's in it for me?" In business, it is so important to find employees who want to help themselves. Self-motivators, people who look for challenges and for ways to better themselves, are the best people to hire to work in our offices, factories, and service-oriented businesses.

Uncovering promise in your employees is a talent that needs to be developed. It doesn't come from opening a book, taking a test, and then claiming to be an expert. Understanding how to draw out the best in those around you is a gift. So the question lingers: how can the positive attributes of the worker be uncovered?

Because I feel this is important, I am returning back to Maslow. He stated that the highest of all the needs, self-actualization, is the quest of reaching one's full potential as a person. He also believed that as a person becomes more identity cognizant, the person would also gain more wisdom. As a result, the person would better know how to handle a greater range of circumstances.[8]

Just like you (as I tried to point out in a glaring, incisive fashion), employees have a need for reaffirmation. During a casual chat or a formal performance evaluation, think about ways to articulate positive feedback to all members of your staff. Tell them what they are doing well and what you would like to see them work on to be even better. They'll be grateful for your sincerity and will work harder to not let you down, if your actions support your words. Everyone has a particular talent, so it is your obligation to find a way to use that talent for the good of your company. If your secretary has a propensity for specifics, then consider using her to manage a particular project you are working on. Why would you even consider looking outside if you have the answer right in front of you? If you do not promote from within, this tells your employees that you do not value them; in essence, you are ignoring their need for esteem.

How a person feels about themselves has a tremendous impact on how they perform. The greater a person's sense of self-esteem, the more confidence that person has in his or her ability to deal with life's challenges. Employees want to know that, if they are contributing to the company in a positive manner and the company is profiting from their toil, they will be recognized and appreciated for that effort. All too often, employers are quick to point a finger if something goes wrong and too slow to say thanks when business is booming. For the same reason that customers buy your product or service—because you persuaded them to do so—employees will work hard for you. It all starts with how they feel about themselves, and if they are getting the consideration, esteem, appreciation, and sense of accomplishment from you, the person they are working to satisfy, they will do their best.

As stated previously, anything that draws a parallel to associations

8   Davis, Stephen F., and Palladino, Joseph J. *Psychology*. 5th ed. Upper Saddle River: Prentice Hall, 2009.

with others symbolizes a relationship to social needs. New employees simply want acceptance, and it is just good practice to include them, immediately, in any type of workplace function to help them become acquainted with their new coworkers. Let me warn you against something, though: don't go to bed with any of your employees. Although shared happenings will help to inspire your employees and meet a need of belonging in a social setting, this is one shared happening you should seriously avoid.

There are many ways to develop rapport with the employees you need to be successful; you can build a tremendous team once they realize that you are using people from within to accomplish business goals. Your staff will understand that you are watching and waiting for them to prove themselves so they'll get an opportunity, and your credibility as a supervisor will skyrocket. As an added bonus, the feedback you receive will be optimistic and encouraging. Today's employees want to be nurtured, inspired, and recognized for their achievements, and they want to feel a part of something great.[9] Your mission is to improve your ability to do that and bring about success for your company. In the end, it's possible you will be on the receiving end of a good review and possible promotion.

A leader's character, or lack thereof, also provides insight to the business itself. In order for your business to be profitable, you must be truthful and principled yourself. Paying attention to client relationships and placing their needs above all others is the first step in engaging in business integrity. Customers, both existing and potential, will gain a great deal of respect for a business that pays attention to their needs. When you, as a manager or supervisor, show this type of commitment to the customer, you will also gain much respect from your employees which will make them want to follow you and trust in your ideas. But beware; if you are simply providing lip service to any of them, they will eventually see through you and you will have a difficult time regaining their respect. Commit this to memory: whether they are customers or employees, do not associate with people who lack character and place their personal interests above those of the people that place faith in them.

---

9   Gallo, C. *10 Simple Secrets of the World's Greatest Business Communicators*. Naperville: Source Books. 2005.

Chapter 6
Free Thinking Is Something You Make Them Pay For

An idea that is developed and put into action is more important than an idea that exists only as an idea.

Buddha

When did having a mind become a detriment to good business? As a supervisor, are you so insecure that you believe smothering the ideas of other people is better than remaining open to the suggestions of others? I'm sure that when you were a small child, someone probably told you to shut your mouth and commented that your ideas were ridiculous or silly. You're not a child anymore, though, and it's now time for you to grow up and act like you have a freaking brain—and let your employees use theirs as well.

Think of how our quality of life improved because of people who were not afraid to think outside the box and ask the important "what if" questions. Alexander Graham Bell was probably ridiculed when he decided to create a system of communication that traveled through an electric wire; Ben Franklin may have had some odd looks when he decided to fly a kite in the rain with a key tied to it; and Philo Farnsworth, who invented the electronic television, probably received some cross-eyed looks when he said it was possible to show moving images through a piece of glass. These people, and others like them, dared to ask, "What if?" What if we made it bigger, faster, hotter, colder, or cheaper; what if we charged more or made our company more relevant? Do any of you inane managers allow your workforce to use their minds to help you succeed or do you take every opportunity to curtail free thinking? You should know that these "outside the box" employees can add tremendous value to your business if you allow them to, because their questions could spawn solutions to your business dilemma.

Being blessed with a creative mind is a tremendous asset, and having the ability to use that creativity for the betterment of your business is an even greater gift. But we know why you don't want employees to think: it is because people who do may object to the status quo, and their questions could reveal your true lack of knowledge. If you would take the time to encourage creativity among your workforce, you will foster a more innovative environment that challenges them and allows them to do more research on their own so as to produce better results for the business.

Creativity makes it possible to construct distinctive relationships where they may not have existed in the past. With so many resources at your disposal, one of your inspired employees may find a way to reach another customer segment for your business, devise a new advertising campaign, refine a product, or improve your department. As a manager, you can use the tool of creativity to gain an edge over others in your company who refuse to think out of the box.

So let's make this simple: taking advantage (not in the negative sense, you idiot) of free-thinking employees could help you solve a problem that you haven't been able to solve yourself. And to think, this all begins with communication. Another quick lesson for those of you who slept your way into your positions or slept through your college classes: communication is an exchange of ideas between two or more people. That is about as simple as I can make it for you. One person isn't dominating the process; communication is a forum for everyone to share thoughts or ideas. When someone else is speaking, you have the *obligation* to listen to them. You may not agree with them, but active listening, which is trying to process what you are hearing instead of thinking about what you are going to say next, will bring great rewards if you are willing to put it into practice.

Discernment is another important factor in the communication process. It is the process in which we decipher specific details about our surroundings. Supervisors with an ineffective communication style create strain in the entire organization, which affects the relationship between management and staff; this strain often emerges as a focus of exploration in various contexts.[10] You should realize that every member of the company is a unique creature with individual dispositions, behaviors, and personas.

If you can develop this insight, you will find that it can improve your credibility. Managers need to get away from established standards. Many feel like they have to force their principle onto others rather than taking into consideration that everyone has a great deal of knowledge to offer. Developing the proper insight and treating everyone as unique individuals will help you avoid lumping them into a category of expendable servants; it will also help you overcome the fear that you are not up to the job yourself.

For any business to be profitable, employees at all ranks need to communicate effectively. Basic courtesy between the sender and receiver of information will aid in establishing better working relationships. Allowing each member of the organization to convey thoughts, feelings, knowledge, and information through speech, actions, and writing, using proper channels of communication, will open avenues of awareness that can be rewarded by your branch becoming more productive and innovative.[11] Does this really sound like something bad?

Remember, it should be accepted as common business wisdom, and implemented as part of any strategy, that employees want their contributions to be seen as essential to the success of the company. Creating a free-thinking environment in which workers are allowed to express opinions and offer suggestions promotes an innovative, vibrant workplace which allows everyone to participate with other

10   Mawr, Bryn, "Individuals and culture." 2009.http://serendip.brynmawr.edu/exchange/individualsandcultures (accessed April 16, 2010).
11   Wild, J., Wild, K., and Han, J., *International Business*. Upper Saddle River: Prentice Hall, 2008.

members of the organization in a variety of occupational endeavors. It is also a way to show you have faith in them and prove you trust they want to be productive employees, capable of fulfilling your requests, all with the hope of moving up in prominence within their profession.

Some of you may be greatly offended at my name calling or finger pointing; creativity should not be just some out-of-control opportunity for ideas to be tossed around. It ought to be combined with critical thinking processes to break down and separate various aspects of a problem. Giving each of you the benefit of the doubt that you can actually handle this task, you should be able to get to the root of the reason for the business dilemma you are dealing with in a more efficient way.

Business is about solving problems. Solving problems means your business will have a better chance to produce more revenue, and the more revenue you create, the more likely you will succeed in your career. Being able to think freely allows your employees to be innovative, which, in turn, improves the chances that you will find the best solution for your business. Like it or not, people are the key to a successful business, and we all need to treat each other as we would like to be treated, including the chance to articulate ideas.

Chapter 7
Know Your Role

Do not worry about holding high position; worry rather about playing your proper role.

Confucius

As a manager, you play a vital part in devising a strategy that attracts the brightest and most promising employees as well as creating plans that keep current talent on your roster. Training and development systems keep current employees motivated, with the understanding they have the opportunity to grow and flourish in a company that takes interest in their professional enhancement. But some organizations allow unskilled managers to show favoritism, misuse systems that are designed to provide quality customer prospects to each employee, or place unrealistic demands on employees when common sense should prevail.

So, with all that being said let me point something out: you need to know your role, since you want to act like an expert in all areas. When you are acting in lieu of an actual HR professional, you should conduct yourself like a professional as well. One of the missions of any supervisor is to alleviate the problems mentioned and to follow organized and efficient HR practices. By making use of sound procedures that follow state and federal guidelines, you can be sure that your efforts are in compliance with all laws and sound business practices. As a result, you can avoid conflicts that stem from differing opinions about job responsibilities, and your enhanced training procedures will enrich workforce production, morale, and, dare I say it ... even *your* performance.

Throughout this section, we will look at specific areas of concern and discuss ways to improve them. Staffing and training and development will be the main focus, with some attention paid to leadership, which is often an overlooked quality. Results are not guaranteed, but the domino effect can be expected to produce favorable business results, which should lead to improved revenue and new business potential. Wouldn't you like for your supervisor to see you as a valuable resource that helped contribute to the success of your business? Pay attention and maybe you will learn something that could make that happen.

One of the central concerns that managers have is hiring procedures. Using inconsistent hiring procedures can devastate your business. By following an efficient hiring routine, you can reduce legal risks that can result from perceived bias, prejudice, unequal treatment, and discrimination. In addition, making foolish hiring choices could increase employee turnover and decrease consumer retention rates. What is a foolish choice, you ask? Well, let's look at one foolish practice.

Just as favoritism between supervisors and employees can lead to problems in the workplace, hiring practices can also generate negative results. Hiring friends or relatives implies that you are more concerned with having acquaintances close by or are trying to win points by employing those close to your superiors instead of candidates who can help turn out new business. Also, while you may win some short-term approval, you had better hope that they can deliver long-term success and keep existing clients at ease. In the event that your new hire is a close associate of your supervisor, you should also be sure that they do not report back and are trying to take your job as well. Yes, folks, it's a sad but true statement, but there is no honor among thieves. You would be better off taking the time to hire the best qualified person who fits in with your organization's mind-set and objectives. Once you do make your selection, you should then be sure they are all treated fairly and have a desire to please you without feeling the gaze of acrimony upon them. Showing respect for your staff will help you accomplish this purpose.

As a way of creating more cohesiveness and to avoid legal problems, conduct yourself like a principled HR professional to eliminate any employee-related rifts. Some benefits of this strategy are diminished costs, enhanced efficiency, and better workforce morale.

Speaking to each of the benefits, costs can be reduced due to improving the hiring process. This is achieved by bringing on more qualified individuals while eliminating the perception of "it's who you know, not what you know" in the hiring process. Costs decrease when supplementary training is no longer necessary for extended periods; new hires who are qualified can get into production quicker. They will enhance efficiency and eliminate downtime and sluggishness resulting from overworked employees carrying the burden of inadequate staffing, which should also lead to improved morale.

From your management point of view, avoiding these poor administration practices should free you to concentrate on more important areas of your work. If you do not have an HR background or the skills needed to thoroughly examine candidates, try to assess if the potential employee will fit into your company's culture. The onus is on you to develop a better aptitude for the obligation that you claim to be capable of, but have probably failed at; hence the reason someone bought you this book. A simple hiring process you can follow, once streamlined into a well-organized ritual, may include these simple steps:

1. Establish need
2. Offer internally (if applicable), post externally
3. Screen applicants
4. Interview applicants
5. Analyze gathered information
6. Choose one or narrow field for secondary interviews if necessary
7. Notify each candidate of results (an often overlooked piece)

Inconsistencies can have a devastating overall effect on a business when it comes to training and development of personnel. Imagine the impression that is created when employees are given varying bits of information and then asked to do a task in a consistent way. Employees are usually not incompetent individuals. Most are college educated and have a high degree of knowledge and passion to offer. However, issues are created when questions arise that conflict with the training an employee has received.

Morale is reduced when employees are chastised for making a mistake or not following a particular protocol even though they are doing exactly as they were taught. Over and over again, an employee may ask questions regarding a task but they may be given different directions than they were originally trained with. Employees trying to gather enough information to be more effectual may even be met with a ridiculous comment such as, "If I have to do your job for you, then why did I hire you?" or "What do *you* think you should do?" Sadly, if you reply with comments like this, you probably couldn't do their job anyway. You are a bona fide incompetent that is undeserving of your position because they are asking for help. But more often than not, this circle of disorganization repeats until a solid worker ultimately leaves, when all they wanted was to be trained a bit further in something that could help them help you.

The customary challenges associated with revamping a training and development process, nevertheless, will come from managers who want employees to do things in a particular manner, since that is the way it always has been done, instead of taking a moment and offering a bit more (particularly with supervisors who are afraid to ask questions that may bring about positive change, since they don't want to draw attention to themselves). Consider for a moment that maybe the training program didn't cover all the issues employees face. For this reason, you might be called upon to offer a bit more in the way of employee development. If you are not sure about an answer, then you should say you don't know before asking someone else for clarification. Your questions, concerns, or comments might help improve the company's instructive resources. Since change may not be easily accepted within an organization, even if it's necessary, you could be viewed as an agent of positive change that modernized the organization.

Managers responsible for employee development need to remember that using proper training methods, understanding learning styles, and being aware of the various methods of delivery all help overcome the challenges associated with these tasks. Lee Iacocca, when asked about problems Chrysler was having, once said, "All of Chrysler's problems really boiled down to the same thing. Nobody knew who was on first. There was no team, only a collection of independent players."[12] This book could help you see the need for change in your behavior and help you realize the important role you play in business success, not only as a manager but as a mentor, teacher, and business partner.

Finally, the economic impact on your organization should be significant in view of the fact that employees, both new and existing, will receive training that is in harmony with company goals. Managers who have a negative bias toward their company, the training process, or a trainee are capable of doing more harm than good. By ensuring that everyone is properly trained, productivity and morale will improve, which will increase revenue as a result of uniform performance standards and the ability of each employee to work in a manner that is well defined.

The morale improvement will be evident in less absenteeism and improved overall performance. To be clearer, morale is related to production in the following way: performance is determined by employee morale, which can be described as the spirit of a person or group as demonstrated by confidence, cheerfulness, self-control, and eagerness to carry out assigned tasks.[13] With the understanding that morale is an influence that stems from the top down, helping others understand the need to buy into the philosophy is a key to enhancing

---

12   Harris, K. "Managing conflictTechCom Manager". 1. 15 (2005), http://www.enewsbuilder.net/techcommanager/e_article000492611.cfm?x=b11, 0, w. (accessed November 13, 2010).

13   Fink, N. "The High Cost of Low Morale." *The Leading Edge 3*, no. 1 (2010).

the revenue aspect of the new strategy.

A poll by Gallup calculated that losses of more than $270 billion per year are attributable to employees who are dissatisfied with their jobs. Low morale results in enhanced work absences, lost productivity, and poorer health due to stress.[14] Each of these issues, with many more not mentioned, is cause for concern and can be rectified if a more reliable approach to training and development is implemented. Wouldn't you want this kind of improvement attributed to you?

This data should inspire each of you to do whatever is necessary to ensure your workforce is content and feels as though they are respected, valued, and appreciated. By paying attention to the details in this area, employees will have a better mental focus and attitude, which will automatically compel them to want to perform at higher levels. To be clearer, it has been estimated that the value of a publicly traded organization, on average, increased 16 percent when their workforce boasted a higher morale in contrast to those companies that sported lower morale.[15] This point should be common sense, but I will ask it anyway; as managers, isn't it more advantageous for you to be a reason that profits increase instead of one of the reasons they decrease?

As stated throughout this segment, there are several factors that can create a more inclusive environment and improve your business. Leadership is a key to being successful in any area where employees look toward others for guidance and direction. Those who are in management positions must possess leadership qualities, encourage the workforce to bring questions and concerns to their attention, and give them feedback so employees understand their role in the organization. These qualities will also improve the chances for career development and mobility within the organization.

What many fail to realize is that a new hire's attitude, with respect to duty to an organization, begins the very first day. The impression they get, based on their treatment from managers and

---

14   Esty, K., and Gewirtz, M. "Creating a culture of employee engagement." June 23, 2008. http://www.boston.com/jobs/nehra/062308.shtml (accessed November 21, 2010).
15   Dive, B. "Why organization design is critical to global leadership development." April, 2005. http://www.conference-board.org/topics/publicationdetail.cfm?publicationid=957 (accessed October 7, 2010).

other employees, is significant from the moment they begin. Mentors and trainers, the first important faces the employee interacts with, are a key factor in the success, or failure, of the new employee. Even long-standing employees will seek out these experienced voices in order to get their questions answered, so it should be obvious about why this is such a crucial moment in the employee's work life. The mentor could turn out to be a treasured role model during the initially perplexing entrance into the network of the organization. By ensuring this initiation is done successfully, you are building an insurance policy that will provide rewards for a number of years, and as a manager, you take on the role of a *leader* who is not afraid to admit that you just might not have *all* the answers but you have the ability to bring people together for overall company success.

Chapter 8
If You Won't Think about Your Employee, Think about the Customer

There is only one boss: the customer. And he can fire every-
body in the company from the chairman on down, simply by
spending his money somewhere else.

Sam Walton

Our society is based on customer service. Regardless of the type of commerce one is involved in, customer service is a crucial part of business success. Because of the competition in nearly every market, customer expectations are increasingly more stringent and continue to expand every day. In today's economy, people are looking for bargains at the business-to-consumer level as well as business-to-business. In order to survive economically, attention must be paid to this vital area since businesses look for bargains just as consumers do. Good service professionals *might* stay alive, and those who place emphasis on this subject significantly enrich their chances.

Analyzing your business's customer service effectiveness should be done methodically. Comparing your location to another without looking at other factors is a sure way to bring a business to a standstill. The concept of "one size fits all" may work at McDonald's, but not all companies fit this methodology. As an example, your business may offer home remodeling that is guaranteed to be done in one day. On the surface, it sounds like a great way to enhance the look of a home and increase its market value. So why wouldn't someone want to take advantage of something like this if it can result in a greater return on their investment? The answer is simple: demographics. This is the problem I have with managers who simply manage instead of being proactive and taking the initiative to delve into the deeper areas of business development.

When a business is not producing the desired results, it is easy to point fingers at the employees; many poor managers do this. More often than not, the real issue is never addressed unless managers do the work necessary to acquire the information needed to be successful; instead, they would rather point fingers at the easiest target: the people that *appear* to not be doing their jobs. I emphasize "appear" because staff members are usually working as hard as they can with the tools they have. Sorry, people, more has to be done, and this is where you need to get off your lazy rears and be proactive.

This is done by clearly defining the problem and sharing it with others in the organization. As a quality supervisor, you can do this by asking questions of those who hear what your customers are saying on each phone call or at each face-to-face interview. This will be the first step in implementing a plan to fix the problem.

The next step is to determine your target market. Earlier, I mentioned comparing yourself to other locations, and now I'm going to tell you why it is a bad idea. Although both locations may appear to have similar demographics, there are other variables to consider. Issues such as income level and unemployment rates are important, since cost may be an issue. Household size may also well weigh in as a dynamic for practicality, and age might be a factor (some age groups will not find your product or service sensible). More breakdowns can easily be done, but resolving the problem should be the first order of business. Knowing this information will help determine the best person or department to fix the problem.

As mentioned, defining what the problem is will help you implement a course of action. Identifying where the conflict is occurring will show you where you need to pool your resources when you present the ideas to your supervisor. Examining a customer's service history, such as who your penetrated audience is, what the trends are in your industry, and who your target audience is, will give you a better chance of overcoming your obstacles. You simply have to get over your fear of those above you in order to make it happen. If your supervisors are anything like the parasites described throughout this book, then maybe you should provide them with a copy also.

Your metrics could tell you how long the crisis has been brewing. This data will help the organization reevaluate their approach to an area because, unfortunately, failure to meet the challenges listed may have already resulted in the company's reputation being harmed as well. Finally, learning exactly what the problem is will permit you to recognize what performance standard is missing. You already know that customers are unhappy, or you wouldn't be paying attention to these issues now, but the silver lining is that this gives you a starting point for alleviating their concerns.

Now that you have determined that your employees may *not* be the chief concern and the problem is clarified, your next step will be to set a goal. Setting a goal will ensure that you have a defined objective to work toward. Industry standards vary because each business has their own way of doing things. They also have their own idea about what makes a company successful, so they tailor their plans to meet different objectives. Your purpose should be to remain profitable while providing your patrons with the product or service they need. Classifying goals in a primary, secondary, and consequential way will help you to set priorities. As you improve one area, other areas should improve also. These are known as secondary metrics because they are desirable performance side effects.[16]

Finalizing your plan involves choosing who will direct various functions of the plan; identifying and planning for problems along the way; having a strategy to proceed; and performing an assessment of your line of attack. Since the scope of your project may be large, it will be important to have people in position that can help facilitate the assignment. Upper-level management has to be informed of what you are trying to accomplish. This will shift the onus on them to help you obtain the data needed to develop into a more profitable business. *Do not be afraid to present it that way either!* You are supposed to be

16   DeCarlo,N. *Lean Six Sigma*. New York: Penguin Group, 2007.

a team that is working toward one common goal. Remember, nothing worthwhile is ever easy, so get over your insecurity and get in touch with those who can help you achieve this goal.

Commit this to memory so customers understand that you attach importance to their concerns; communicate your objectives to them with the sole purpose of improving their ability to get what they are demanding. This also helps to avoid any gridlock that may occur in your business transformation. As in any relationship, communication is the key to success, and this approach will demonstrate that you are not blind to their concerns. Your corporate office or owner should be happy with your initiative to lead (there's that word again) the charge to improve your area.

Department supervisors are typically the main ingredient in making a business plan successful. Like it or not, you are the eyes and ears of the organization, as far as your corporate supervisors are concerned, and only you can provide the much-needed insight as to what is the most efficient way of meeting customer demands. Upper management must understand if you have to hire more people or if you simply need to combine various tasks or departments to become more efficient. Your employees can help determine what is critical to meeting the requests of your customers as well as providing you with credible data that allows you to forecast the expectations your supervisors will, in due course, hold you accountable for. Using the knowledge they possess can be beneficial in making a plan that is pleasing to your customer and your corporate partners.

Just a little side note for you: your corporate partners are those above you, and you should look at them as such instead of being fearful of asking questions or taking the initiative. Quality, delivery, and price are important to your clients, and the biggest concern you should have is finding a way to deliver the message to your target audience that the product you offer is worth their investment. You simply cannot do this alone, and by alienating your employees, you risk failing to meet your operational goals every time. You can continue to point fingers, but eventually the microscope will be on you, and the staff that you lose in the process just might be the same people who are helping their new employer obtain the customers you helped to drive away.

Your ability to be viewed as a customer-friendly organization begins by simply reacting to their concerns in a positive manner. Remember, *you* are not the point of contact for the customers, your employees are. It is your obligation to listen to their concerns and then, if you have doubt, do some research on your own. Who said you can't pick up a phone and ask questions or listen to the customer yourself? Now, before you give some wise-ass answer about why do you need your employees then, consider this: your willingness to get into the trenches will speak louder to your leadership capability than anything you can utter verbally. Communicating that you are working to fix the issues that create anxiety for the business is the first step in ensuring you keep your customers loyal and hopefully drum up new business due to the word-of-mouth advertising they may well do for you. Taking the methodical approach that has been described will ensure that you do so successfully while providing quantitative results.

Chapter 9
Managing *Your* Performance Needs

*A manager is responsible for the application and perfor-
mance of knowledge.*

Peter Drucker

Throughout this book, I have called out those of you who are the typical workplace bully, the insecure underachiever that beats your chest to intimidate others who may possess more talent and knowledge than you, and the ignorant fool who believes that when you were given your position, you were bestowed with all knowledge and wisdom as a result. In this chapter, I am going to take a different approach; the sole purpose of this book is to help you realize how valuable your staff members are. You have to reconsider your approach because, eventually, your mismanagement will be the cause of your ruin. The people who work for you actually want to please you and want to be a vital part of the company's success. Just because they are motivated is no reason to keep them down by trying to sabotage their career or their potential to move up in the organization. So, with that being said, pay attention to the following information because it can bring you great dividends if you apply the information to your management repertoire.

For companies that do not currently have performance management systems in place, adding such a new system can create problems. Implementation of any new practice can be a great source of anxiety. Most people are creatures of habit, and even when changes are made to benefit them, they may still find it difficult to accept. A performance management system may be seen negatively by those who fail to see the need for it. Usually, these people are afraid that their underachieving work habits will be exposed. For this reason, performance management systems can have a positive benefit by their mere existence.

We'll discuss performance management a bit further, but before we do, it is worthy to note that defining what constitutes poor performance is not as easy as it may sound. Some people say that if you don't make a certain number of calls or reach a certain sales objective, then you were a poor performer. I have to differ with this view, though. If the goal of your business is to reach potential customers, then what good is it to repeatedly call a disconnected number? Wouldn't it make more sense to send those potential customers a letter or an e-mail? If your employees take time to do that but it interferes with time on the phone, then shouldn't you recognize their effort for trying to generate business?

Performance must be gauged alongside some criterion or projected level of success before it is considered inadequate or effective. There should also be some type of standard deviation based on averages and, I'm going to go out on a limb here, *realistic* expectations. I use the term *realistic* because many managers are not competent enough to forecast wisely, and they, in turn, create unrealistic projections that are impossible to attain. This is not an excuse to not reach new heights in business objectives; I am simply stating that many of you are not skilled enough to make accurate projections, and you place undue pressure on people who know what is rational.

Career development is an often neglected but indispensable feature to help produce a useful performance management system. Managers often focus on appraisals that are designed to rank employees. Although they are a necessary evil, these appraisals can have a negative effect, such as lower morale and higher turnover, which can be devastating to net revenue. They can lead to employees feeling that the organization is more concerned with money than people. Businesses exist to generate profits, but if care isn't taken to incorporate employee needs into the equation, the outcome could be damaging before a potential star is able to shine. Eventually, this type of practice spreads into the employment-seeking community, and you may find it difficult to acquire top talent and retain the people you already have. The key is to harmonize business goals with individuals so each has an opportunity to mature, with the end result designed to be an elevated degree of employee allegiance and sustainable, enduring efficiency.

If your company does not have an encouraging organizational structure, employees will feel that it is simply a greedy institution that could care less whether their business approach put an end to one's occupational drive. Your workforce will have the point of view that they are worthless and insignificant. The end result for a business is lower productivity, diminished concern for the company, and clients that will take their business elsewhere.

Employees may be a terrific fit for an organization, but their talents may not be used in the appropriate area. By reassigning them to another part of the business, there is a strong likelihood that they could be re-energized since they will believe their value is being seen by those in charge. Care must be taken to ensure that problem employees are not being passed off to someone else, which is an entirely different issue. By bearing in mind that the majority of workers have a desire to perform effectively and improve their livelihood, proper incentives ought to be presented to them. Encouraging outcomes will be realized by both employer and employee in view of the fact that each takes a more involved interest in accomplishing collective goals.

Ranking and rating systems are also a valuable performance management tool. It is actually a very useful way to evaluate the performance of employees; however, care should be taken to still look a bit deeper into why a worker may not be meeting company metrics. If you want to base decisions simply on numbers, then this is an effective way to gauge performance in comparison to others. Since it is a numbers-driven tool, it is a quantitative method that can be used to evaluate employees. Managers need to be skillful enough to evaluate the entirety of why one employee is meeting objectives while another is not. An old adage states that "all that is red is not roses."

Using the analogy, I warn against making rash decisions based on numbers, because you may lose an actual star while retaining another employee who has far less talent.

Scaled rating techniques are arguably utilized above all other evaluation processes. The main reason is that they are relatively effortless. Some of these rating techniques bring into play percentages based on interrelated business functions such as leads, calls, contacts, and meetings. Others are more simplified, resembling sliding scales of 1–5, or extremely dissatisfied to extremely satisfied, and so on. The capacity to work within time constraints to a perceived level of competence can be rated by scaled evaluations.

The flaw in this approach is the fact that the system is subjective; bias, partiality, or unfairness can easily figure into a worker's appraisal. Whatever the case may be, the goal is to arrive at a consistent and impartial conclusion. This is why it is important that managers be trained if they are going to evaluate their workforce. It is a key area of employee development; even greater significance ought to be placed upon the impartial measures for promotion as opposed to character qualities or the perceptions of potentially biased supervisors. Removing the subjectivity will give employees the impression that they have as much likelihood to be successful as anyone else.

Subjectivity should not be allowed in the workplace; it uses unethical conduct to negatively affect the professional well-being of another staff member. Managers who engage in workplace harassment by showing favoritism in the workplace do lasting harm to a company as they damage the company's reputation and could force productive employees to leave. This is why I feel it is so important to only place people in leadership positions if they have the qualities of a leader, instead of promoting someone based on the mere fact that they did a good job in their area of expertise. A person who may not perform well in sales may be an outstanding fit in another area of the business. It makes no sense to move someone who is proficient at one thing to another area, especially if the two areas are dissimilar. It's like asking a star quarterback to shift to center, which brings me to the next topic.

Ironically, when a person is promoted to a supervisory position, they are often taken from one area of the business in which they were successful and moved to a different position that does not allow them to use their natural abilities that permitted them to blossom in the first place. Competent performance management calls for adept communication with members of the workforce on a more personal level. Interaction is a key ingredient to help you understand the competency of your employees, and if you fail to get to know your employees, then the chances of directing them to produce in a more fruitful manner is effectively diminished, and production suffers. The key is to be certain that managers, both new and experienced, are properly trained in the skillful art of motivation, teaching, and articulating company goals, and they must understand the needs of their employee to allow them to reach these objectives.

To bring the necessity of proper performance management into perspective, successful business managers view the appraisal process as a means of becoming better acquainted with those who work for them. The reality of the situation is that managers frequently place too much emphasis on who wins and who loses each week's sales or production targets. There is no doubt that promotional and earnings enticements are essential, but it should also be remembered that they are merely a small fraction of the broader plan. As stated earlier, the human element is a key component of business success. Regrettably, many companies ignore the value of having an adequate performance assessment system that can teach just as much as it grades your workforce.

As I mentioned, management needs to be skilled at delivering the right message to their employees. The message takes the form of coaching, change in the workplace, or business goals and expectations. The entire performance management procedure means nothing until it is actually put into practice. It is simply empty words until executed. The practice can easily be destabilized, however, when it is conducted with a haphazard approach. There are several things that you need to bear in mind as you learn to deliver the message:

1. **Be encouraging.** You should strive to persuade employees to *want* to be better. Tearing them apart will only foster more animosity and resentment, which is not conducive to a productive work environment.

2. **Engage in a sincere conversation.** There is a difference between talking *to* someone and talking *at* them. Feedback will allow each of you to understand the other's point of view and come to a resolution of concerns.
3. **Use good judgment.** Some people, despite their outward demeanor, have poor self-esteem. Openly admonishing them or publicly chastising staff members, either individually or in groups, can damage your workers' attitudes in addition to creating an us-against-them situation when, all the while, each person should be working as a member of the team to bring about one common goal: company success.

Company managers should be blazing the trail toward constant group efforts. This important part of corporate culture begins with skilled guidance, and communication is a key component to ensuring it is done effectively.

Remember, it is important to have a process in place that allows each employee to be successful from the moment they are hired. Failing to implement a uniform process opens the door to litigation, which could cause a financial disaster, not only from the legal aspect but also from the perception that is created within your business community. As has been pointed out repeatedly, training and development are continuous functions; they do not end once an employee is through the probationary period. The needs of the customer are always changing due to motives that are wide ranging. It is crucial to a company to know that employees are given every reasonable accommodation to improve their performance based on these variables and to train them to recognize, and react, to each in a constructive manner. Once all resources have been exhausted to allow them to improve their performance, then alternative channels can be used as a means of corrective action (up to and including termination, if necessary).

Chapter 10
You're Not Qualified to Ask Questions

Accept business only at a price permitting thoroughness.
Then do a thorough job, regardless of cost to us.

Arthur C. Nielsen

The saddest part about this section is that it brings into a very clear light that we do not live, or work, in a perfect business world. There was a time when families believed the company would always take care of them; however, those days have gone by the wayside, as evidenced by repeated corporate scandals that have cost hundreds of thousands their jobs and brought a large magnifying glass onto corporate America. Since the theme that we have been talking about has been the lousy manager, I will stay on topic, but with this bit of understanding: all employees, both managers and their workforce, typically bring baggage with them into the workplace. The baggage stems from individual pressures we face, defects in our character, or traits we learn spending too much time in front of the TV. Regardless, all workers have their share of trouble, and it can be the source of workplace conflict; it is up to the employer to eventually designate who is to blame. This is where corporations can become remarkably flawed as they refuse to look at the managers who may be justly to blame for the troubles the business has to contend with.

As a manager, you should be aware of *selective attention,* which, in HR terms, is defined as *not* paying attention to what is going on in order to placate corporate desires. This unjust disposition often reveals itself as an ineffective investigation that does not get to the core of employee issues and tries to encourage the complainant (usually the employee) to drop their complaint or make them believe it has no merit. The end result is that stricter rules are levied for a period of time in a manner that almost surely will result in the employee's subsequent termination later on down the road.

Shoddy, indifferent examination into issues can result if the investigator does not take the time to speak to potential witnesses or other affected parties. This style of selective attention can induce investigators to form a silent opinion that compels them to side with decision-making partners instead of actually trying to get to the root of the problem. Employees may well be suspicious and pessimistic toward the investigator. It should go without saying that because these disagreements could possibly have a bearing on their ability to make a living, the employee might yet be cautious with all the facts (how's that for being polite). On account of these reasons, problems between employees and managers should be completely and thoroughly looked into to establish what really happened or where the problem truly originated.

I'd like to tell you that workplace investigations are a quick and easy fix to your problems, but they are neither quick nor easy. There is no magical procedure that will help you perform investigations in your office. They are all different because the issues, people, and circumstances are all unique. As in anything else, some problems can be exposed swiftly and unobtrusively, whereas others might involve a very extensive evaluation of the whole management team.

It is very important that whoever is conducting the investigation should protect one key player in this unfortunate game: the accuser. Even though you may suspect that the complainant is being vindictive, you cannot be sure until a thorough examination is complete. Complainants typically believe they have a very legitimate issue and are seeking assistance from the only resource they have at their disposal: the HR department. If you are responsible for conducting the investigation, you should not have the idea that you are simply going to do what is best for management while ignoring the facts.

If you ignore this important phrase, a *pattern of behavior*, then you are going to open the company up for further litigation. Every now and then, managers that you may perceive as being fair or impartial are the problem you need to address. Their exasperating actions are going to eventually cause the organization a great amount of unneeded distress because, generally due to a conceited attitude, they do not seem able to stop. More often than not another employee is able to see the pattern of unjust management, and is often the victim of it. It is because of this that many choose to litigate their workplace issue instead of working them out, since the impression is that administrators are all in bed together. Even if your company wins in court, the average cost to defend a case is roughly $250,000, while settlements average approximately $200,000. The damage to a company's reputation in the court of public opinion can be even costlier.

The problem with most HR people is that they do not have any clue as to how to investigate a claim, other than the knowledge they gather from watching shows on television. How often does an investigator tell a suspect they are being investigated before taking the time to gather all the information they can from the victim? The answer is, rarely. Unfortunately, in many companies, that is exactly what happens. An employee files a complaint, and then the first (unwritten) action is someone from a corporate office informs the accused that one of their employees is stirring things up. This allows the managers to start preparing their defense and gives the HR person some time to gather negative data about the complainant. In all actuality, the *first* person that needs to be addressed, in an absolutely impartial way, is the accuser.

When the investigator speaks to the complainant, it should be done in person and in a confidential, safe location. This will prevent the appearance that the company is trying to eliminate the "trouble maker," which is probably on the complainant's mind already. There are rare instances when someone will lodge a complaint simply because they have a vindictive personality and want to create turmoil, but more often than not, complainants are using this forum as a last resort. They may have already tried to rectify the problem by speaking with others, but to no avail. Any notion to the contrary on your part is inexcusable and shows how careless you are; you must conduct a fair, thorough investigation if you want to actually make the company a better place.

Complainants should be allowed to disclose their version of the issues as they see it. Asking open-ended questions is a great way to begin the process, but you should allow them to get their story into the open asking specific questions. You have to remember, the complainant is under duress and may not be too trusting of anyone in the corporate chain at this point. Once the problem has been described in their words, then you can go back and draw out the clarifying details. Personally, I don't recommend gathering complex details over the phone. There are too many distractions and areas of concern that can be brought up if the case goes to court. These issues often could cost someone their livelihood or reflect poorly on the company, so take the time to sit down and conduct a face-to-face interview. If the complainant hasn't done so already, have them write a thorough account of the situation. Be sure to inform them of the process and how it can be expected to unfold.

The next step should be to interview any witnesses. This could substantiate the claims being made or may show the allegations to be uncorroborated, either of which helps the investigator to determine what steps need to be taken next. Typically, the next step is to interview the accused and allow them to respond to the accusations. Only then should they be allowed to gather their supporting data, if any, to reply to the complaint. Once that information is assembled, then the investigator can follow up with anyone they feel is necessary to help come to a successful resolution of the issue. This is the only justifiable way to conduct a serious investigation. Properly attending to and exploring employee complaints can help to enhance worker relations as well as avoid court findings that have the potential to be costly in ways beyond money.

If you are a manager who is reading this book to learn from other people's mistakes and do not engage in the behavior that has been portrayed throughout, congratulations. You probably have a solid workforce that has very little, if any, of the issues we have discussed. Please remember this one point, though: other managers may be the cause of the problems you are having. It may be easier to treat the labor force as an expendable commodity, but eventually the continuous turnover is going to have a negative effect on your business. Don't be afraid to make changes in the managerial ranks. You may find that your workers are actually terrific people who can greatly enhance your company's effectiveness, but they were being held back by lousy management. Remember, if you conduct an investigation that reveals serious problems, you have the responsibility to do the right thing for *any* wronged staff member, whether it is a manager or everyday hourly employee, or face legal or civil consequences.

Chapter 11
Time to Get Fixed

*Good people are good because they've come to wisdom
through failure.*

William Saroyan

Although we're really not referring to dogs in this chapter, many managers need neutering from the leadership point of view. They don't seem to understand that generating a culture of distinction in a workplace involves more than simply practicing good management principles and applying sound leadership (which you may not be doing anyway). It is about instilling in employees the need to work to benefit the one tangible asset that can make or break the organization: the customer.

But employees who repeatedly face adversity due to incompetent and uncaring supervisors are not going to be able to fully concentrate on that one asset. With that in mind, in order to promote the mission of the company, those at the top must make clear directives so that each staff member understands the commitment that must be made, which will then trickle down to the attitude employees have toward clients and customers. After all, who can really concentrate knowing that nothing they do is ever going to be good enough? If you are capable of making positive changes, then a first-rate reputation will emerge. This reputation then becomes an asset that will be part of the company and is the first step in a proactive plan.

People with perfect eyesight are said to possess 20/20 vision. It is also the best description of hindsight. Being proactive involves using mistakes from your past, or the mistakes of others, to avoid future problems. It means taking initiative, and a great way to avoid problems is to have a standard operating procedure (SOP) which can be tied into the policy manual. The difference between the SOP and policy manual is that an SOP explains a course of action to carry out a particular process or development action or in response to a specified happening and a policy manual typically encompasses pay, benefits, performance expectations and legal issues.

Most of you probably already have some SOPs set up in your workplace. If not, you should consider creating an SOP to be part of your business strategy, as it will help you avoid obstacles and legal problems. If your company has procedures in place, you should evaluate them. A comprehensive evaluation could help your company adapt if business storms result from employee negligence, management incompetence, or economic issues. The SOP serves as a beacon for a business ship to steer toward in an ethical crisis as well.

In contrast, a reactive approach may serve as a costly reminder that plans should have been made ahead of time. There is a risk in allowing events to determine the business plan. Don't wait for something to happen before making contingency plans. Hasn't there been enough history to draw from to motivate you to develop an individual response to various situations? Managers who mistreat their subordinates may be unaware of the need to use more diplomacy, but the reality of the situation is that their company must now proceed in a hasty manner because they have allowed certain behaviors to continue.

It's easy to look at various metrics and say the employees are not pulling their weight, but what if the work they are doing is reflective of the leadership (or lack thereof) they are getting? Is it really fair to punish those who are only doing what they are told, and in the manner they are made to do something, when the problem lies within the crap artist who bears the title of supervisor? It is also easy to say that employees are lazy, but that does not take away the need to have a plan in place to avoid situations such as these.

With a reactive approach to business, there is no beacon to guide the lost business vessel. It must fight the choppy waters with the hope that it does not crash against the rocky, legalistic shore that can prevent it from taking to the water again. If you are an inspiring executive who wants to be even more successful, you should consider that your management team may be the problem. Don't simply assume that they are the golden children and can do no wrong. What you may be left to deal with is constant turnover, which also contributes to low productivity from added training time, loss of production, or even a lawsuit based on wrongful termination due to a crap weasel making your HR decisions.

I'm not trying to say that you will not come across a bad egg that needs dealt with, nor am I saying that you should place all the blame on your managers, but identifying the problem is the first step in the decision making process. If an entire unit is missing their target goals consistently, then you may have an issue with the person leading that team, which you should consider *before* getting rid of handfuls of employees at one time. If it's only one or two that continue to struggle, then, after taking some corrective measures to try and get them on the right track, they may be the weak link. But once identified, it is important to produce options and then take action. This step will compel the leader to view the dilemma from various perspectives so as to make the best decision possible. Some ways to generate solutions include the following:

- ✓ Brainstorming
- ✓ SWOT analysis
- ✓ Means and ends examination

Keep in mind, this is something that you should have already covered in various business courses; nonetheless, once the various alternatives are settled upon, it is important to look into the risks, preferences, and repercussions that may result, and then select the choice that is most suitable for the situation. After you choose the best option that will help solve the problem and avoid future missteps, check the decision so you can state that a logical approach has been taken and to make certain that the course of action is not tainted with miscalculations. SWOT analysis is a wonderful line of attack for business problems. This methodical technique will help you assess the plan at every stage. This will make your company more competitive; you will make calculated, contemplative decisions to help the company succeed in a gradually more aggressive global market.[17]

Finally, it is important to communicate the decision to all members of the organization that will be influenced by the choice you make. Communication is a vital component of effective leadership, and by informing others why a particular choice was made, it will be easier to garner support. Making available details concerning risks and anticipated advantages will add credibility to the choice made.

You may need to make a presentation supporting your decision; my suggestion is to put together a special project team to obtain the necessary facts to present to those who are touched by the decision. Although this may create an unexpected expense, the consequence of not taking action could result in a contentious situation, which may perhaps become more costly. Pursuing excellence is different for each company. By taking these precautionary measures, it indicates to your employees, shareholders, and clients that you know what is expected (excellence); are not afraid to admit there is a problem (many of you bury your pin-heads in the ground, hoping the problem will go away); will commit to solving the dilemma; and will strive to motivate your employees in a extraordinary way. It is a way for you to practice honesty, even when it hurts, since leaders should strive to tell the truth and do the *right* thing at all times.[18]

In summary, looking beyond the basics can have a significant impact on your business. You will be seen as a conscientious manager that values your employees and customers; you also will avoid the costliness of potential litigation and loss of reputation and future

17   Coulter, M. (2008). *Strategic Management in Action.* Upper Saddle River, NJ: Prentice Hall.
18   Daly, J. (March 2010). *Creating a culture of excellence.* Retrieved from http://www.entrepreneur.com/magazine/entrpreneur/2010/march/204984.html

customers. If you don't believe that a reputation can be tarnished, I encourage you to research such examples of loss of reputation by simply looking at a few of the for-profit career colleges and the negative websites devoted to them. A proactive approach will help avoid many problems. All you have to do is ask yourself what will likely happen if you take a certain action and then respond to it prior to the occurrence. That proactive approach is an invaluable investment in you, and your company's, future.

Chapter 12
Don't Overlook Policy

A good plan implemented today is better than a perfect plan implemented tomorrow.

George Patton

Now that we have resolved many of the issues you have on a personal level, let's discuss a valuable tool that you can reference to avoid problems you probably experienced in your haphazard approach to management: your policy manual. Reliable business guidelines endow managers with the structure to aid in governing employee relations. These guidelines are an invaluable means to help a business navigate the often difficult and stormy sea of employer/employee interaction, and a well-crafted policy manual will allow both managers and employees to gain awareness about expectations and avoid confusion in the workplace. You still need to be aware that differences of opinion may require interpretation in some areas of policy, so if you are writing a policy manual or adding to your company's existing guidebook, make sure that your ideas are clearly written down and conveyed to your workforce.

There are numerous reasons that you need to be a part of initiating change. If your market has seen a growth of competitors, your best chance to succeed is to be proactive in your business approach. Economic factors often have a bearing on who will succeed in an industry. Companies that are hesitant to turn out goods or services with lower prices or are unable to show customers why their products are better than the competition will have a problem surviving without review their current goals, objectives, and approach. As a manager, you have the duty to report these issues to those above you and to ensure you are doing everything in your power to stay abreast of trends in your area. Many managers fail because they refuse to take the extra steps necessary to verify what their target audience is capable of or willing to support.

Before you make an argument about the quality or value of your product, let me remind you, the customer will determine what is valuable. They are the people who are buying, and their perception is the noteworthy factor in your success. Perception can be reality if the pocketbook is making the decision, so if you do not take the time to do research about your targeted demographic, then you have nobody to blame but yourself when you fail. Your employees are a critical component to ensuring that you are able to meet your business goals, so I recommend you look at, and use, them as an instrument to help you succeed.

You may ask how you are to make this happen. First, let me remind you of something that I stated earlier in this book: you must have enough courage to state your concerns to your supervisors and not be afraid of asking for help. Nobody expects you to know it all, and if they do, then they are the type of people who need this message more than you do. I can tell you that, as an employer, I am often too close to the situation to see all that I should. Oftentimes, I react emotionally to a situation, and I need the eyes and ears of my loyal employees to aid me in obtaining a proper view of the condition. For this reason, I welcome the advice and input from those who work for me.

If they merely tell me what they think I want to hear, then I lose respect for them; they are not doing me, or the business, any good. I don't want a bunch of butt-kissers surrounding me; I want inspired people who want to provide the best possible information so we can improve as a team. My suggestion is that many of you should read that last sentence about two hundred times. I would hope that your supervisors would have enough respect for you that they would be willing to listen to the ideas you present, or to offer suggestions themselves, instead of answering your questions with a question. Many people do that because they don't have any answers and are afraid to go to the next level to ask or don't want to appear unknowledgeable to you. Trust me, if you are in the category of cowards I've described, then you are not alone. The corporate world is full of ill-mannered and unqualified, self-proclaimed leaders. These are the people who may have been good at the job they were pulled from before being placed into a supervisory role in which they have no experience or understanding of how to succeed.

You have to take a *leadership* role to be the type of manager needed to make the changes the company seeks (I do suggest you go back to the section about being a leader and read it again). Transforming a business requires attentiveness throughout the change process. Incorporating the human resource dynamic is a great way to acquire the information you need to be successful. By only paying attention to the development and execution elements of your business, you risk creating an air of opposition to any proposals. It is an indispensable requirement for you, the business manager, to approach your ideas with a well-thought-out point of view so your evaluation, planning, communication, and management approach is successful throughout the life cycle of the initiative.

This repeats what has been stated in earlier chapters, but it bears reiterating: friendly communication is a vital component of change management and ought to stretch to all managerial echelons. In order for you to be respected as a leader, you must develop your communication skills. Your workforce will be more compelled to contribute ideas and offer feedback when they are confident that you want them to be part of the process. Allowing your employees to take a hands-on approach will make them feel part of the problem-solving process; it also permits you to exploit their personal familiarity, which may help to contribute to your issues in a positive manner.

Training should be a fundamental element of your policy initiative. Without guidance and enlightenment, it is nearly a futile undertaking. Training allows employees to understand why a policy is being changed. By making this a routinely proactive approach, your workforce will gain a greater awareness as to why this change will improve their work environment.

Care should be taken to avoid messages such as "You are prohibited from …," because it may be offensive to a workforce that consists of experienced, responsible, and ethical individuals. You, as a manager, have to remember that morale is one of the workplace intangibles that must be considered, and offending your employees can have a negative effect on morale. By including an open discussion period during regular training times, everybody on your team gets to be a part of the change; you will be able to gauge their reaction and discover potential obstacles (remember the proactivity referred to before), and the open dialogue allows you to be recognized as an involved, concerned supervisor rather than a egghead who could care less.

Next, instituting performance benchmarks will help to quantify your business goals. The benefit is to allow you to present a well-thought-out deliverable and then align the wherewithal to make them reachable. This helps your employees to understand what is expected and lets them track their progress. When a request for much-needed feedback is phased into the equation, the data can help you produce effective and lasting change at a quicker pace. The end result is that you, as a supervisor, will become more respected among the workforce, your employer will see you as a more constructive asset, and the area you manage should be increasingly profitable.

Chapter 13
The Result of Your Negative Approach

Of all the attitudes we can acquire, surely the attitude of gratitude is the most important and by far the most life-changing.

Zig Ziglar

As you watch a large number of employees continue to walk out your door, you should realize the negative financial implications their departure has on the business and your ability to meet company objectives. There are numerous reasons why companies experience high turnover rates. One cause that does not reflect as negatively on management is that more and more employees from the baby boomer age bracket are retiring. As these skilled workers leave, companies are having a difficult time finding experienced people to replace them.

Another cause of turnover, which may be more attributable to poor management, is employees who are constantly searching for extra money or better benefits. For this reason, it is becoming fairly customary for people to change employers on a more frequent basis instead of rooting themselves in one company, as was commonplace in the past. Money is often the cause, but there is another issue that can make it more difficult to acquire new talent: lack of proper supervision.

We have talked about this throughout the book, but it bears repeating: employees are the people who will make or break a business. It is their effort that will make it look good or bad. Poor supervisors take the credit for the efforts the employees make and may unfairly criticize those who work for them. For reason such as these, employees would rather take less money and work for someone who values their effort than work for someone who is unappreciative. Workers simply want the opportunity to grow professionally and be respected for the exertion they put out.

Turnover, although something that is not entirely preventable, characteristically falls into two categories: separation expenditures and replacement costs. Severance pay, outplacement costs, and legal fees resulting from involuntary severance fall into the separation expenditures. Replacement costs are incurred during the hiring process. Advertising the position, screening candidates, conducting tests, and the interview process all contribute to the cost of hiring. Other replacement costs may include signing bonuses, relocation costs, and orientation and job preparation expenses.[19]

Besides the monetary issues associated with separation and replacement, there is also the concern of lost productivity and the process of indoctrinating new employees into the company culture. Revenue may well decrease in the event sales go down due to clients who were attached to the departed employee. Since many customers develop a good rapport with people they work closely with, it is a very real concern. This problem may continue even after a replacement is hired, since there is never a guarantee that people will get along, so group dynamics become an even greater concern. If this aspect is not adequately managed, then the potential for repeated turnover becomes an issue. First-rate management is the key to this component being successful.

As a means of being proactive, it is in the company's best interest to carefully garner the opinion of the workforce. Employee

19   Greer, C. R. (2001). *Strategic Human Resource Management*. Upper Saddle River, NJ: Prentice Hall.

satisfaction surveys are a good way to assess workplace attitudes, but care should be taken to ensure anonymity. Employees are likely to be reluctant to submit opinions if they think they will be passed along to others, who may retaliate. The best time to conduct these surveys is when the mood is light so as to remove the emotional aspect. Many workers react emotionally, and their answers may be reflective of a recent incident or event that caused distress. By allowing for a cool-down period, answers may be more honest rather than an expressive flare-up.

Another way is to simply observe. If you really want to see how people feel about their jobs, you should watch their behavior.[20] Those who are enthusiastic will ask for more opportunities or even take the initiative on their own. Workers who are simply being compliant may do only what is asked but with no zeal or obvious delight. And people who are simply collecting a paycheck may detach themselves from their peers, take more breaks, complain more often, and produce less because they basically don't care.

Finally, by reviewing company history, it is possible to notice periods in which the turnover rate was at the highest. By studying the demographics of the people who left the organization, you can avoid hiring others who may fit the same profile. Evaluating periods of high turnover periods can help you change your approach in order to help retain personnel. Regardless of which method is selected, and I recommend all three be used, the information gathered can be an invaluable resource for the company.

Employee turnover is an important issue that should be examined immediately. It is the everyday worker who will make, or break, a business. Although these employees are being paid to do a job, they are important resources that should be recognized as a vital component in the wheel of corporate achievement. It is their effort that ensures products are properly manufactured, customers are treated fairly and respectfully, and revenue streams continue to pour in.

Just because they work for you does not mean their morale shouldn't be taken into consideration. The greater a person's sense of self-efficacy, the more confidence that person has in his or her ability

---

20   Heathfield, S. M. (2010). You can reduce employee turnover. Retrieved from http://humanresources.about.com/od/retention/a/turnover_tips.htm

to deal with challenges pertaining to work.[21] Your support will help to ensure their loyalty and, perhaps, enable your company to generate more revenue. For this reason alone, doesn't it make sense to build up their spirits? By using the assessment tools previously mentioned, you show them that you care about their work environment and automatically meet one of the needs that every person has: the need to feel respected.

As you show your employees that you understand their workplace needs and their feelings toward work, you also increase the likelihood that they will be more efficient for you. More efficiency means increased monetary returns. Improving your supervisory skills can therefore reduce employee turnover rates and help your business prosper. The financial result of repeated turnover can be grim for a business's bottom line. Managers, business owners, and CEOs need to be aware of turnover's pricey impact and spend time contemplating ways to retain their top staff members (or any employees that have potential to be noteworthy contributors). By behaving more respectfully toward your employees, turnover and grievances will be indisputably lessened.

---

21   Davis, S. F., and Palladino, J. J. (2009). *Psychology*. Upper Saddle River, NJ: Pearson.

Chapter 14
A Final Thought

*First comes thought; then organization of that thought
into ideas and plans; then transformation of those plans
into reality. The beginning, as you will observe, is in your
imagination.*

Napoleon Hill

Throughout this entire book, I have talked a lot about your failures
as managers and your lack of ability to be a true leader. The purpose
of this has been to make you realize how others perceive you and
your approach toward them, with the hope that you will change your
behavior. I trust that you actually do care about how you are viewed
by others, although you may never have taken a step back to consider
how your actions may contribute to these perceptions. You may not
have even realized that your conduct has resulted in failing to meet
your business goals.

Many of you have worked for people who fit the description of
the harsh incompetents that have been portrayed throughout. I urge
you to take some time and reflect about that experience and then ask
yourself, do you really want to be like them? You are trying to do your
job to the best of your ability, but your skill is being overshadowed by
the neglectful attitude you show those in your charge, which is then
exposed via poor production or lost revenue.

I have no doubt that you have talent. You would not be in your position if that were not the case, but you can be better; we all can. Every one of us is looking for our "pursuit of happiness" moment, where our supervisor looks at us and says, "Wear your good shirt tomorrow because it is your first day of work, if you want the promotion." Do you want the job—the chance to make a difference, the opportunity to fulfill the dreams you had as a child that you haven't been able to realize yet? You are the one person who can make the unseen element of business success more visible—culture. How you lead others becomes evident in the type of employee you see in the office every day. Your proactive approach, and the ability to put it into words, is just one of the steps in being a good manager. You have got to develop your capacity to persuade and influence in a positive way before you can hope to implement your ideas.

I have overlapped a great deal of information from one section to another, with most of the overlap concerning communication and leadership. These are two of the most important ingredients of being a successful business manager. You cannot lead effectively without communicating successfully. Transformation is much easier when you are able to communicate your ideas in a manner that garners understanding, and understanding enables you to gather support. As you inspire, you generate a feeling among those who are going to carry out your request that not only are they enhancing the business, they are also bettering themselves.

Don't confuse your personality with your ability to lead; you do not have to be charismatic to be an effective leader. Having charm is nice, but it is more important to know that your employees have confidence in you. You develop this confidence when you treat others with respect, allow them to see that their opinions do matter to you, express interest in their concerns, and treat everyone fairly, without subjecting them to skewed bias.

Being flexible is another trait of a good leader; you must develop this attribute since you are dealing with a diverse collection of personalities, each with their own preconceptions that are formed long before you ever entered their life. With so many cultural distinctions to be aware of, you should remember that what is considered normal in one region may have a negative implication in another. People bring these cultural norms to the workplace, and you have to be cognizant of the differences. The key to becoming a better manager, however, is respect. If you simply demonstrate for others the same consideration that you would like to have, then you will be on your way to becoming a better manager and on the road to developing into an esteemed leader as well.

Chapter 15
Some Additional Help

Never wear a backward baseball cap to an interview unless applying for the job of umpire.

Dan Zevin

I hope this book helped you transform yourself into a productive business manager. If it did not, then you may have been ushered out of your place of work and need to prepare for another career. In the unfortunate event that happens, I am including some standard interview questions to help you prepare for your next assignment. For those of you tasked with the hiring process, these are the types of questions you should ask potential employees. I have included sample answers so you have some guide to use as you prepare for your interviews. I recommend that that you do research on your targeted job so you can craft your answers to fit the job you are seeking. Remember, these are only samples of questions that you could be asked, along with illustrated answers. It is in your best interest to examine yourself so as to provide the best possible response to an interviewer.

Why are you interested in this job? This is a great career opportunity, but even more than that, the job seems tailor-made for my skills. I'll be able to put my proficiency in marketing to work here, and it will be exciting. My interpersonal skills are well suited to me meeting and speaking with new people.

Why should we hire you? No matter how much groundwork is done, every now and then things go wrong. I keep my head when the world around me appears to be falling apart. Not all problems can be dodged, but the most important thing is to take care of them quickly and calmly when they happen. Not only that, a lot of people probably have a similar skill set, but I have a terrific ability to cope well with conflict due to my diverse background. So not only can I do the job, but through my approach I am able to contribute to a positive work environment, which is important.

How do you manage/handle pressure or stress? Some people shy away from it and pretend it doesn't exist, but we all know that isn't realistic, so I embrace it. Pressure and stress are part of the working world, and I thrive under pressure. I bend but I don't break.

What are your weaknesses? I have the propensity to take on too much at one time, which places more self-induced stress on me. To counter that, I now like to make lists, which I check every morning, to make sure I stay on track, and I block out periods of time on my daily calendar to keep my time more organized and efficient.

Tell me about a time where you had to deal with conflict on the job. Our boss didn't understand the work we did and, as a result, demanded procedures that were outdated and ineffective. Everyone in the department complained about the problem, so one day I suggested we explain things to the director. We did it as a group, but I drew up a marketing plan consisting of the outdated procedures in contrast to the proposed new ones, showing how those saved time and gave better results. Our boss thanked us for the explanation but still insisted we do things her way, stating that the new procedures were well thought out but that the company had been doing things the same way for forty years and she didn't want to go against what they had already come up with. I understood her point of view, although the plan could have allowed us to identify our target audience and improve our organizational endeavors.

How well do you work with people? Do you prefer working alone

or in teams? I enjoy working as part of a team but also on my own. My career has allowed me to do both. I read the job description on your website and figured that there are going to be opportunities to do both, and I look forward to each one. The bottom line is I meet goals.

What can you do for us that other candidates can't? I am an excellent coordinator and project planner, even for complicated issues. My communication ability and my experience in reaching the target audience gives me a distinct advantage, because I am able to enhance the mission of the institution.

What was your greatest professional accomplishment? (Explain something that has been a great source of pride for you as it relates to the job you are seeking.)

What five adjectives describe you the best? Ethical, empathetic, self-motivated, reliable, hardworking. (Find the adjectives that best fit you.)

How would you evaluate your ability to deal with conflict? I try to take the perspective of walking a mile in another's shoes and try to see things from their viewpoint. So when there are differences of opinion, I look at the situation from the other side. This approach allows me to be a team player; I am willing to consider other opinions, which is also an important component of leadership. I do believe that conflict is best met head on and should not be overlooked.

How would you describe yourself? (This is an area in which you need to explain how your character will benefit the company in an efficient manner.) I persevere. I continue to strive toward reaching my "pursuit of happiness" moment. This opportunity is a part of my pursuit. I spend time trying to figure out how to make things work so I don't let others down, but in the end, it's all worth it. I'm not here to live a selfish lifestyle; I'm here to care for those that have been entrusted to me.

How do you measure success? I evaluate success in several ways. At work it may be meeting goals while sustaining a wonderful working relationship with coworkers and customers. At home, success is the satisfaction of my kids becoming successful and making good decisions. Success is relevant to the setting I am in at that moment.

Why do you want to work here? My research showed me that this company is an industry leader and recognized throughout the area. I see the potential for me to become part of a terrific organization in an industry that I truly believe in and consider it a perfect match for me and what I want to do. In a nutshell, I want to be involved with (insert company name).

What qualities do you think are necessary to make a success of this job? (This is an area that you will have to review in order to determine if you are capable of meeting performance requirements.) Outstanding communication skill; ability to research and seek out opportunities for growth; ability to promote the mission to a diverse collection of potential clients; diversity appreciation; well written and spoken.

Have you ever had difficulty with a supervisor? How did you resolve the conflict? (It is important to remain positive although this question opens the door for you to provide a negative response.) Our boss didn't seem understand the work we did, and as a result demanded procedures that were outdated and ineffective. The definition of insanity is doing the same thing over and over while expecting different results. While it seemed we practiced insanity, I concurred that I would follow the directives although I believed other alternatives were available to help each team member be more productive. As a result of being able to air our differences of opinion, we worked closer as a result. Remember, you can always agree to disagree. You may even decide that, in the end, it is best for you to go your separate ways without being critical.

How would you define a good working atmosphere? I believe an environment that would allow me to sharpen my existing skills and increase experience to aid in my career growth is one. Also, one that promotes teamwork and cooperation among the different departments in order to realize objectives would be a great environment to be involved with.

How would you describe your work style? When something has to be completed, I get it done. But it's not something I rush, it's attention to detail and to quality. It's not just a job done, but a job done well due to the fact that I believe in doing things right the first time. I strive to learn as much as I can to make myself an asset to my employer. I don't consider myself smarter than other people, but I do put in a lot of extra effort and clearly identify objectives so I can accomplish and, hopefully, surpass them. And finally, I like to plan things and then stick to the plan, but I know that sometimes the best plan needs to change on the fly. It's actually part of good planning to be flexible, which I try to be.

What did you dislike most about your last job? I never really considered anything about it to be distasteful. It was a satisfying experience to have worked with the people at that location. Everyone got along, knew their jobs, and was willing to help each other when someone needed it. I look forward to similar encounters here.

While trying to meet a cut-off date, you discover a snag that will delay the finished result. How do you handle this? Although I do well working under pressure, I fully understand time management techniques and always build in sufficient time when managing any project to allow for delays of this nature. Time management skills are an important part of being successful and productive.

What is your personal mission statement? To keep my feet firmly planted in reality while never forgetting that good dreams lead to great achievements.

When were you most satisfied in your job? I enjoy the challenge of troubleshooting problems and helping others find an answer to issues they can't seem to manage on their own. When someone else doesn't have the answer, I love helping them come to a solution. It's something I'm genuinely good at as well.

If you are hired, what will you do in your first thirty days? I want to spend some time learning as much as possible from the person I work for and having them mentor me in the new position so that I will be fully prepared to handle all the duties when I take them on myself.

I would also like to spend some of that time getting acquainted with the staff that I will be working with and learning as much as possible about the business operations. On the other hand, if I will need to hit the ground running, so to speak, then I will spend time, before assuming my role, learning about your needs so I can be effective from the day I begin work.

At the close of your interview, you may well have an occasion to ask questions of the interviewer. I have listed a few of the standard clarification questions you might want to ask.

Do you have questions about the job/company?

1. How do *you* describe the job and its responsibilities?
2. How many people work in the section where I will be working?
3. Is there travel? If so, how much?
4. What do the typical work week hours look like? Is overtime expected as a norm?
5. Are there opportunities for growth and professional development?
6. Does the company pay for, or reimburse, any continuing education?
7. What do you like about the business?
8. What don't you like about it?
9. If I am offered the job, how soon would you want me to begin?
10. From this point, what is the next stage in the process? How long before I hear from you, and through what means?
11. Is there a dress code and what is it?
12. Will there be supplementary interviews?
13. Do you have additional questions for me based on anything that I have asked?

Good luck to each of you and please visit http://kennetheugene-consulting.com whenever you need a trusted associate to help you handle your HR business concerns.

References

Clark, Donald. "Concepts of Leadership." 2008. www.nwlink. com/~donclark/leader/leadcon.html (accessed June 9, 2010). Coulter, M. (2008). *Strategic Management in Action*. Upper Saddle River, NJ: Prentice Hall.

Daly, J. (March 2010). *Creating a culture of excellence*. Retrieved from www.entrepreneur.com/magazine/entrpreneur/2010/ march/204984.html

Davis, Stephen F., and Palladino, Joseph J. *Psychology*. 5th ed. Upper Saddle River: Prentice Hall, 2009.

DeCarlo,N. *Lean Six Sigma*. New York: Penguin Group, 2007.

Dive, B. "Why organization design is critical to global leadership development."April, 2005.http://www.conference-board.org/ topics/publicationdetail.cfm?publicationid=957 (accessed October 7, 2010).

Emerson, Ralph W. "Quotes Museum." 2010. http://www.quotes-museum.com/quote/28412 (accessed January 2, 2011).

Esty, K., and Gewirtz, M. "Creating a culture of employee engagement." June 23, 2008. http://www.boston.com/jobs/ nehra/062308.shtml (accessed November 21, 2010).

Fink, N. "The High Cost of Low Morale." *The Leading Edge* 3, no. 1 (2010)

Fitzgerald, F Scott. "The Crack Up." 1936. http://www.quotationspage. com/quote/90.html (accessed December 3, 2010).

Gallo, C. *10 Simple Secrets of the World's Greatest Business Communicators.* Naperville: Source Books.

Greer, C. R. (2001). *Strategic Human Resource Management.* Upper Saddle River, NJ: Prentice Hall.

Harris, K. "Managing Conflict. *TechCom Manager*". 1. 15 (2005), http://www.enewsbuilder.net/techcommanager/e_ article000492611.cfm?x=b11, 0, w. (accessed November 13, 2010).

Heathfield, S. M. (2010). *You can reduce employee turnover.* Retrieved from humanresources.about.com/od/retention/a/ turnover_tips.htm

Schruijer, S. and Vansina, L. "Leadership and Organization Change: An Introduction." *European Journal of Work & Organizational Psychology* (1999)

Mawr, Bryn, "Individuals and culture." 2009. http://serendip. brynmawr.edu/exchange/individualsandcultures (accessed April 16, 2010).

Wild, J., Wild, K., and Han, J., *International Business.* Upper Saddle River: Prentice Hall, 2008.

Wright, P.M., Snell, S.A., McMahan, G.C., & Gerhart, B. "Comparing Line and HR Executives' Perceptions of HR Effectiveness: Services, Roles, and Contributions." *Human Resource Management*, 2001, 111-123.

www.ingramcontent.com/pod-product-compliance
Lightning Source LLC
Chambersburg PA
CBHW022107170526
45157CB00004B/1520